Perfect Neutrals

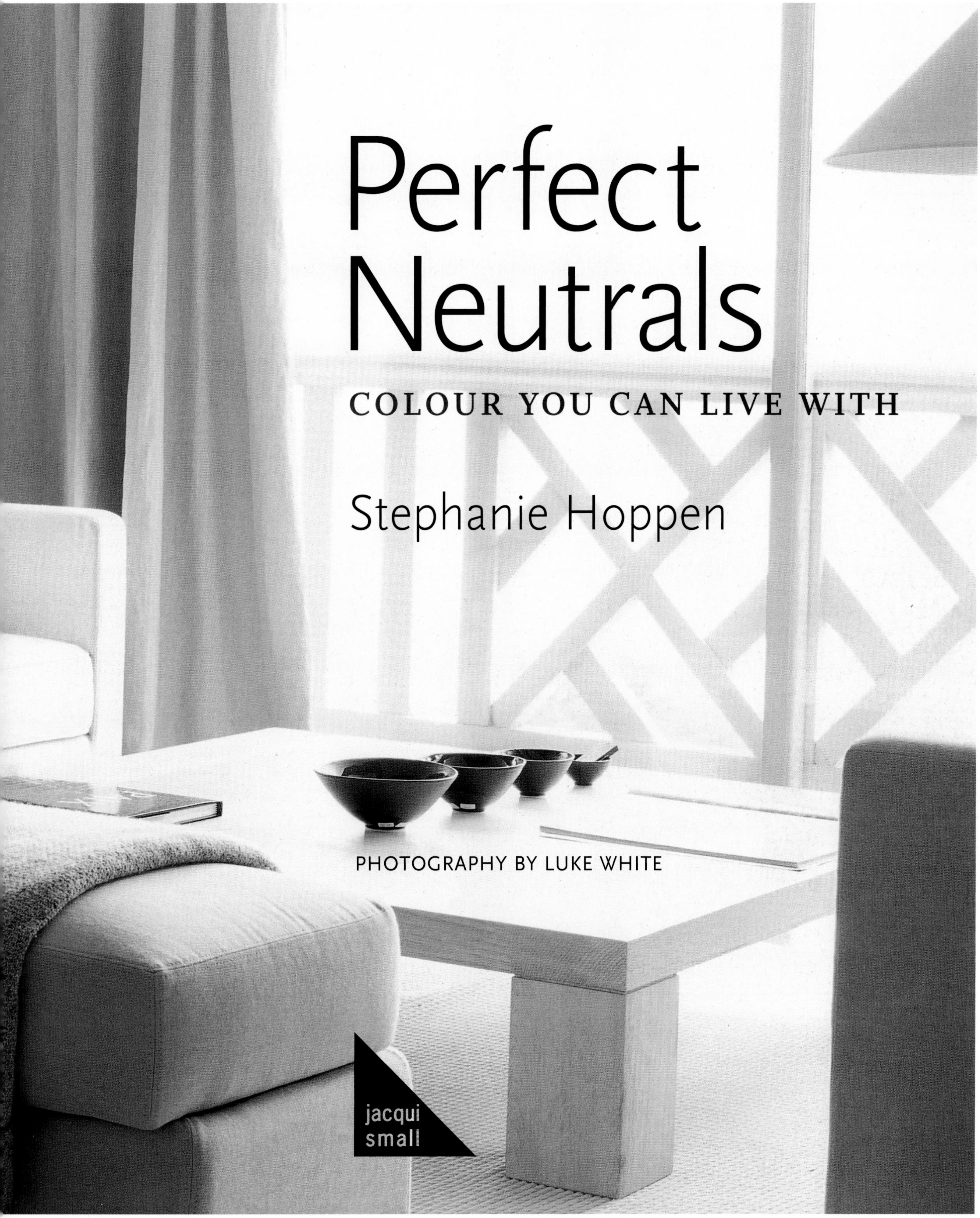

Perfect Neutrals

COLOUR YOU CAN LIVE WITH

Stephanie Hoppen

PHOTOGRAPHY BY LUKE WHITE

jacqui small

First published in 2006 by Jacqui Small Publishing LLP
an imprint of Aurum Press,
7 Greenland Street, London NW1 0ND

Text copyright © Stephanie Hoppen

Photography, design and layout copyright© Jacqui Small 2006

The right of Stephanie Hoppen to be identified as the Author of the Work
has been asserted by her in accordance with the Copyright Design and
Patent Act 1988.

Publisher: Jacqui Small
Editorial Manager: Kate John
Researcher: Pauline Vincent
Project Editor: Zia Mattocks
Art Director: Chalkley Calderwood Pratt
Production: Peter Colley

A catalogue record for this book is available from the British Library.

ISBN 978 1 903221 41 9

Printed in Singapore

Page 1: In Jamie Drake's East Hampton home, a chair upholstered in maize fabric with a terracotta cushion picks out the lightest and darkest tones of the wall behind.

Pages 2–3: To avoid the cliché of an all-cream room, Catherine Memmi has introduced touches of grey – a soft pearly grey throw across the ottoman and four chic charcoal-grey bowls and a charcoal-grey lamp – with textural interest provided by the cream carpet, wicker basket and wooden table.

Page 4: Larry Laslo has made this iron bed supremely comfortable by the addition of sumptuous piles of pillows and layers of bed covers in various textures and shades of coffee and cream.

Page 5 top to bottom: Bernie de le Cuona has created a cosy corner with a sofa upholstered in a brownish fig' linen accented with a rich brown chincilla throw and cushions in white and chocolate suede, echoing the wall behind; the square zinc vases introduce a darker shade of grey into the main living area of Gérard Faivre's Parisian apartment, decorated entirely in shades of pale grey; a serene living room designed by Vicente Wolf features toning shades of soft green alongside various natural woods.

Contents

Introducing the new neutrals

OPPOSITE This earth and spice kitchen by Catherine Memmi is tranquil but without the dreaded overkill of chilly stainless steel. Here you have warmth and old-world comfort but with cutting-edge contemporary design – a perfect kitchen/living area. The warm honey-toned floor and the woven tray contrast well with the deep brown ceiling and units. I also love the textures of the brick wall and generous-sized baskets. The wall is painted in a soft mellow taupe from the same family of neutrals.

RIGHT An example of the perfect layering of tone and texture in a corner of Bernie de le Cuona's living room. The oatmeal fabric of which she is so fond contrasts well with the heavy African bed, used as a table, and the handmade African bowl filled with shells.

WHEN THE WORD 'NEUTRAL' is used about a shade or colour, the image that immediately appears in the mind's eye is of rather dreary, nondescript beige. It is the colour that every estate agent seems to suggest whenever an apartment is bought for rental – 'Oh, madam,' they say, 'paint it cream or magnolia and have beige carpet and curtains.' According to them, this is the neutral world in which most people yearn to live.

Although I love the sense of calm that a pale and neutral colour can evoke, I have for a long time believed that in every colour there are many shades, and quite a substantial portion of these shades are neutral. And in describing these colours as neutral, I mean that they go with most if not all other colours extremely well.

The more I thought about this idea, and the more I looked around and experimented, the more I realized that I was correct and that there is an entire world out there of neutral colours that are not beige. There are, in fact, a host of stunning, exciting colours and tones to be used that add a

completely new dimension to the term perfect neutrals.

The logic of this is apparent as soon as one starts to clear one's mind of preformed ideas and forget about boring beige. For example, if green is not neutral, gardens would always look ghastly; if blue is not neutral, nothing would go with the sea or sky.

OPPOSITE A perfect living space that has been decked out in earth and spice tones that all mix and mingle in a subtle, warm way. Luigi Esposito has effortlessly mixed fabric, leather, velour and faux fur, layering one tone upon another for a contemporary look that never jars.

LEFT A collection of ceramic plates is displayed on this faded grey French dresser. The choice of imperial yellow for the walls and chairs is inspired. It is not a colour one sees often but when used cleverly it brings sunshine and warmth into a room, even on the dullest day.

BELOW LEFT This chair is upholstered in off-white linen and accented with black for maximum impact. The bottom cushion is in a new coal-coloured paper fabric by de le Cuona and sports really smart leather buckles. The top cushion is black ostrich skin – simple and very textured. The neatly folded throw is tribal linen with lovely beads – again adding texture to the scene.

When thinking about which colours are perfect neutrals, forget about the true colours and instead consider the 'dirty' ones. This sounds unappealing, but I don't know how else to describe all those wonderful 'off' shades of every colour that tend to be as neutral as beige but – oh my – so much more interesting and uplifting to live with. When you are devising a colour

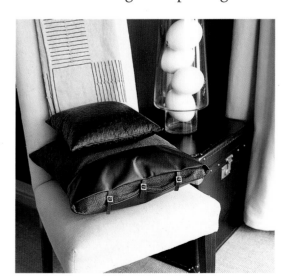

scheme for a room, don't just think about which colours to use, consider how you will use them, too. Think layers of colour in various shades – this can be so effective – and think accent rather than stark contrast.

When all is said and done, what I am saying is that perhaps we need to adopt a new attitude to colour –

RIGHT This exciting,
very French grey
and cream bedroom
has been furnished
with a *lit polonaise* –
one Napoleon slept
in, no less – with the
ultimate luxury of
a superb silk velvet
cover by Edmond
Petit in a rich burnt
orange, a great
neutral as well as a
great accent colour.
Colours that are
found together in
nature will always
be perfectly neutral
with each other yet
never static. Note
the black faux-leather
curtains hanging
from the same rail
as the painting,
below the moulding.
The cream Barcelona
chairs are perfect
side by side under
the cat painting in
similar colours.

OPPOSITE A brick
floor in a chevron
design, glazed to a
warm sand shade,
is a stunning feature
of this outside dining
room designed by
Stephen Falcke. The
walls are in a similar
textured colour,
while the doors and
shutters are a soft
pale grey-blue. Red
is carried through
from the adjacent
room – the old
Transvaal chairs are
covered in a red and
white stripe and the
two French chairs are
in red gingham.

playing it really safe should no longer be an option. What one wants from an interior colour scheme in the twenty-first century is serenity without dullness; colour that does not jar; 'off' shades rather than pure rich colour for the background; and an ability to layer shades of one colour successfully, finishing with a flourish of accent colour that augments and highlights the overall scheme rather than simply contrasts with it in an obvious, brutal way.

As always, I have gone to masters of colour for inspiration, and to find wonderful homes to photograph, and each one of these creative people has added a layer of comprehension and complexity to the original concept of perfect neutrals, helping in many ways to flesh out my initial theories. One of the most significant lessons I have learnt in the course of putting this

book together is how to layer colours and textures successfully. This is such an important aspect of using perfect neutrals, as the soft and gentle rise in tone combined with changes in texture and weight can give a tone-on-tone room enormous elegance and great depth of colour and excitement, while still retaining the sense of serenity that these 'off' colours give. The tone-on-tone concept can be used with so many different shades and textures within a given colour – pale and dark, light and heavy, plain and patterned, smooth and textured, delicate and durable. It is a system that gives a wonderfully interesting perfect neutral base and structure to a room, without ever being boring – or beige. Remember, too, that very dark colours can be as neutral as very light ones. Even more surprisingly, I found that using many tones of the same colour – even a fairly bright colour – can nevertheless provide an extremely pleasing neutral base for a room.

Also key to creating a successful perfect neutral room scheme is using the correct accent colour or colours, in just the right amount and combination, to introduce another dimension to soft, tonal rooms. Accent colours are used to provide visual interest, so they need to catch and startle the eye in a delightful way, but without jarring, seeming out of place or overpowering the subtlety of the overall scheme. Colour accents can be introduced in a variety of different ways, in plain colours or pattern, through cushions, rugs, throws, pieces of furniture, displays of ceramics or other decorative objects, vases and flowers.

Colour is important in life – it can enhance the mood and create ambience – and I hope that through this book I am going to be able to show you how to use colour with confidence to enhance your living space.

OFF-WHITES · Snow Milk Meringue Muslin Egg White Cream Soda Rice Pudding Butter Shortbread Clotted Cream Vanilla Antique Lace Beeswax Biscuit Oatmeal Calico String Almond Linen Stone Twine Distemper Parchment Cloud Coconut Cauliflower Feta Cheese Jute Tuberose Yogurt Cotton Balls Mayonnaise White Chocolate Ivory Chalk Banana Smoothie Magnolia Canvas Mascarpone Hemp Porridge White Truffle

These are the colours, tones and shades that sound and look like comfort food – milk, cream, oatmeal, butter, biscuit. They differ from one another by no more than a hint or suggestion and, as is often the case with perfect neutrals, they all blend together magnificently. These are the colours of purity and serenity. Paradoxically, they can be used to create interiors that are warm and comforting or cool and airy.

This luxurious room by Vicente Wolf features a combination of warm and inviting rich cream fabrics. The buttoned sofa in heavy cream chenille is teamed with a buttoned stool – and here is the twenty-first-century twist – in linen: the same colour but a totally different texture and effect. White gauze linen blinds are paired with silk taffeta curtains.

MILK

EGG WHITE

Larry Laslo shows how wonderful whites and creams can be in a very tailored room. The shades of milky white, in various different fabrics, contrast well with the rich dark wood of the furniture and floor. It is the subtle tone-on-tone colour and texture juxtaposed with the flooring and furniture that bring this elegant room into focus. The absence of curtains means that the view of the fields outside becomes the colourful backdrop.

RICE PUDDING

SNOW TO RICE PUDDING

SNOW

MUSLIN

CREAM SODA

MERINGUE

These palest shades of white are the colours that require textiles to give them depth and warmth, as they need the illumination and grounding of texture to really bring them to life. These pure, milky, snowy off-whites are the colours that the tone-on-tone effect was designed for – building up the comfort factor with layers of tone, texture, weight and colourless pattern can make a room look inviting, warm and elegant, and never dull.

A whiter shade of pale

A ROOM CREATED IN THE palest, milkiest shades of off-white does not need to be monotone but can have surprising richness and depth. Once the base of the room's scheme has been carefully constructed, with flooring, sofas and curtains, for example, many different layers, objects, cushions and accessories can be introduced. These can easily be changed at whim or with the seasons – adding more depth of colour or even rich earth shades in winter, for example, could be a clever way of changing and warming up a room.

These shades of white, though mellow and soft, can be made to reflect many different feelings and emotions. They can be breezy and casual, with plenty of flowing unstructured gauzy drapes and cotton loose covers; they can be cool and no-nonsense, in hard-wearing denim or practical canvas; they can be cosy and comforting in the softest linen or wool; or they can be sumptuous, rich and sensual, in structured heavy silk like a couture gown. Because they blend together so effortlessly, the trick in decorating with these subtle colours is to think texture, texture, texture; thanks to the imagination of some of the fabric designers whose work is featured in this book, as well as the ingenuity of modern technology, we can do this very easily.

The fabrics of Bernie de le Cuona are a case in point. This designer revels in these tones and makes a multitude of them in everything from fine sheer linens to cashmeres and heavy knitted wools, with many different weights and textures in between. I can never pass her shop in London's Walton Street without peering through her window to see what combinations of similar colours but different weights and textures she has used – it is always a feast for the eye and it shrieks simple, elegant luxury and comfort.

OPPOSITE This cool understated room is serene in its absence of clutter. The only accents are provided by the unusual vase by Barovier & Toso on the French acrylic desk and the 1930s Murano chandelier, which add another layer of icy white.

ABOVE Retro padded headboards are very much in vogue – largely because they are far more comfortable than brass, iron or wooden bed frames. This example, along with the warm brown throw, adds another layer of texture to the room.

LEFT A rich chocolate-brown wenge-wood chair by Andrew Martin is given a chic tailored look with off-white linen upholstery and cushions in a combination of striped and plain raw silk. The wall colour is Clunch from Farrow & Ball, a favourite classic background colour of Luigi Esposito.

The snowy or milky colours are stunning as semi-sheer Roman blinds, under heavy silk or wool curtains, or used on their own. They are also perfect for the sheet curtains that are present in most modern homes and look the part in almost any setting. Try hanging three different weights on separate rods, so that they can be pulled independently. Nothing says summer in the country or by the seaside like a floaty off-white linen or organza curtain. Widely available in almost every high street homeware store, these come ready to hang from a pole by a simple tie-top or tab heading. For a fuller look, use three pairs per window instead of one, or use two and let one pair hang loose and scoop the other up with a curtain tie-back.

Egg white, meringue, mascarpone and cream are, for me, the colours of wool and cashmere – gorgeous soft throws tossed over the backs of settees or neatly layered on beds. They add a wonderful sense of winter warmth and cosiness to an off-white scheme, and the more self-patterned and different they are, the better the total effect will be. Layering these colours together in a bedroom or living room gives a secure sense of peace, warmth, serenity and contemporary chic. It can be done in a luxurious way with sumptuous cashmere and fine wools, such as alpaca and mohair, but it can also be done more economically with a mixture of smooth linens, crisp cottons and filmy voiles, which achieves a cooler summery look.

LEFT AND ABOVE This bedroom by Bernie de le Cuona is the perfect example of how to achieve rhythm and balance. This is all about layering many fabrics in the same or similar colours – it's the difference in weight and texture that makes the room gel and ensures that it is interesting as well as tranquil. Pillows, cushions, sheets and throws all lie elegantly one above the other, while at the windows hang three layers of curtains in different weights of linen, all in shades of milky white.

OPPOSITE An off-white backdrop lets the furniture take centre stage. Vicente Wolf has used a dramatic industrial base to support an old plank table – the new industrial chic. The quirky collection of chairs gives this room charm, added interest and a user-friendly feel.

SNOW TO RICE PUDDING TOP TIPS

■ To avoid a lifeless bland old-fashioned look, make sure the colours are layered in a gentle flow, with as much textural difference as possible.

■ Accent with light-reflecting mother-of-pearl, mirror, glass or crystal.

■ Cream linen, in all shades and weaves, can be used to create very different effects. One of the smartest looks is to accent it with black leather, but it also teams well with black cane and natural cane, as well as with stained and varnished bamboo.

■ The relatively recent fashion for stripping, painting and waxing wooden floors is a brilliant idea, especially if the boards are past their best. Look for a creamy or greyish weathered tone for a summery beach house feel – pure white is too harsh. The boards are best left a little streaky and not too even: if they're too immaculate and shiny, they'll give an undesirable 'melamine' look.

■ Lambskin Mongolian rugs are a wonderful floor covering, especially on rich dark floorboards.

This utterly simple white room, where the only pattern is due to the play of light against dark, looks so easy to achieve until you realize that it is all the little touches that make it special – the eclectic collection of objects displayed on the recessed shelves, the understated upholstery, the high white-painted mantelpiece and the black and white photograph resting casually on top of it. Sometimes it is what you leave out that makes a room work.

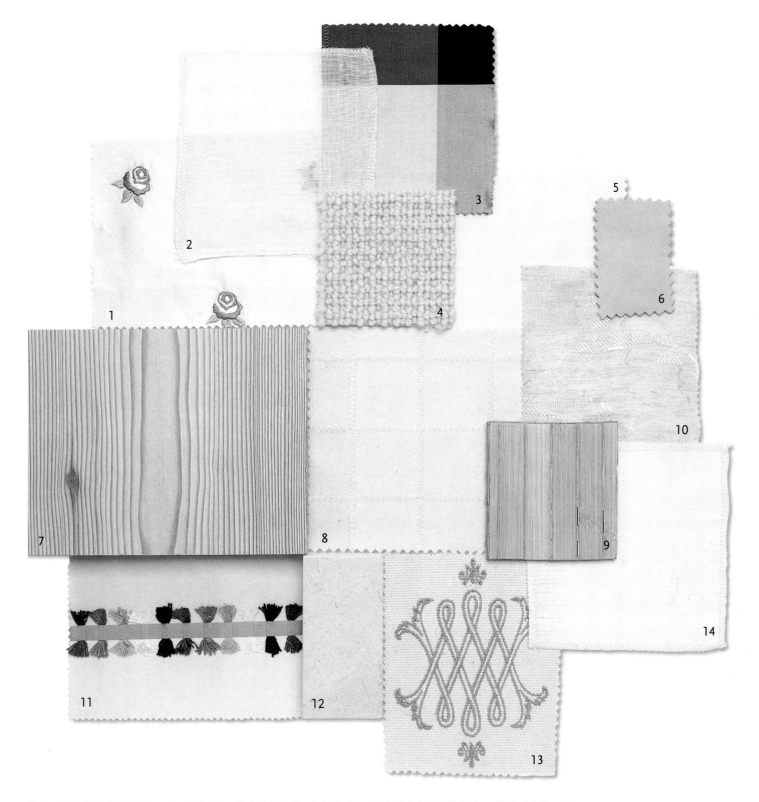

SNOW TO RICE PUDDING SWATCH GUIDE

The most important point when creating a very pale off-white scheme is to ensure that the result is neither boring nor too strident – this is where the tone-on-tone look comes into its own. The goal is a cool, serene space, with an interesting mix of textures to create visual diversity and provide comfort. Try a stripped-down floor in bleached wood (7), bamboo (9) – a great new option – or creamy stone (12), or opt for a wool carpet (4) or a natural fibre such as sisal with a cream-leather edging (6). Add a touch of luxury with a very fine cashmere that would be great for cushions or even curtains (5). Paper fabric (14) provides texture, as do self-patterned designs (8 and 10), while an embroidered fabric (1) or a monogrammed weave (13) would make unusual cushions. The big brown and cream check (3) makes a bold statement, especially if used with another fabric in the same shades (11). It is interesting to introduce the same colours in different designs – using one for curtains and one for cushions, for example. Sheer linen (2) is ideal for blinds or curtains, used alone or layered with a heavier fabric.

BUTTER

ANTIQUE LACE

This relaxed and inviting living room designed by Luigi Esposito and accessorized by Katharine Pooley is painted in a warm cream called Clunch by Farrow & Ball. The wooden floor, wenge furniture, cream linen ottoman and off-white linen sofa are a sophisticated yet simple combination. The velvet and silk cushions in pale turquoise, fur rug, feathered headdresses from the Cameroons and graphic paintings add a softer, ethnic touch.

VANILLA

BEESWAX

BUTTER TO BISCUIT

SHORTBREAD

CLOTTED CREAM

These creamy, buttery colours are the warmest and mellowest of the off-white shades thanks to the strong underlying yellow tone, which gives them their glowing richness. These colours are ideal for upholstery in heavy, luxurious fabrics such as wool, velvet, suede and leather, or for rugs that will help to anchor the room. I think of these shades as 'winter whites' because of the warmth and comfort they bring to a room.

BISCUIT

Liveable modern style

THESE WARM BUTTERY TONES of off-white make a very different interior from the casual, breezy feel of the really pale snowy whites. These are not the colours for beach houses and country cottages; these sophisticated mellow shades are more at home in elegant drawing rooms, in contemporary or period living spaces, or in cosy bedrooms where the comfort factor is high.

These rich colours have more presence than their gauzy cousins and cry out for heavy fabrics, such as sumptuous velvet or wool, shimmering raw silk and luxurious leather and suede. Because they add such a feeling of warmth to a space, I like to use them as 'winter' tones in a paler scheme. Rather like spreading creamy yellow butter on a home-made scone, adding warm biscuit tones to an existing off-white scheme in the form of nubbly knitted throws, velvet cushions or drapes and an area rug, for example, subtly changes the look of the room. This is a great way to create a cosier, welcoming feel for the colder months without spending huge sums of money. In fact, these shades have so much warmth that they almost impinge on the sunny tones, but rest just on this side of the great divide.

Almost all other colours look good in combination with these versatile tones, which are exceptionally smart against both dark and pale wood. Zebra works well as an accent and fur adds to the sense of warmth.

OPPOSITE Luigi Esposito has created a comfortable room with Ralph Lauren sofas, lamps and dark wood table, with walls upholstered in faux suede. The 1930s-style bar was designed by Esposito. The self-patterned paisley linen on the sofas is a good way of achieving a one-colour look.

ABOVE A light-filled creamy living room with gold-toned wooden floor is enhanced by gilt, mirror and glass and brought bang up to date with animal-skin prints.

LEFT Alberto Pinto has added soft texture by covering the walls in stamped woollen panels. The carpet is a cappuccino-froth colour, while the bed and chair provide a coffee accent.

CHOOSING PAINT FRANCESCA WEZEL

■ The most important thing to establish when decorating a room is which kind of finish you want to achieve. If you use gloss or vinyl, the light will reflect off the wall, which will make the room seem smaller. The colour will be flat, without movement, but the reflection will create an interesting effect. A chalky finish will increase the depth of the wall, as the light will be absorbed into it.

■ It is also essential to assess the quality of natural light. If the light is grey and cold, it is not advisable to use brilliant white on the walls because it tends to look grey, especially in the corners. Small rooms with little natural light usually look better painted in strong colours; off-white shades need to contain a good deal of yellow pigment.

An important aspect of any scheme featuring these off-white tones is to ensure that your paint colours are correct. A room can easily be ruined by a cream that is dull or just plain wrong. The choice of colours and paint finishes available today is vast, and sometimes it's easier to choose from a smaller, more select range than from the thousands of shades offered by larger companies. Some of my favourite paint manufacturers are Farrow & Ball, Benjamin Moore, Kelly Hoppen, Flamant and Francesca's Paints, created by Francesca Wezel (see Sources, page 188). Francesca's colours are divine and the catalogues are hand-painted, so you see the actual colour you'll achieve. Her limewash makes walls look appealingly weathered and timeworn.

Almost all companies sell mini pots to try at home. I recommend painting a large area of a wall that gets sunlight and one that does not. View both in daylight and electric light, as the effect can be very different.

BUTTER TO BISCUIT SWATCH GUIDE

Soft gentle floors are ideal for this warmer palette of off-whites. Honey-toned wood such as oak (6) is ideal for living areas, while warm sand-coloured stone (10) is a practical choice for kitchens or bathrooms. A softer option is a textural wool carpet (2). If there is a staircase or long narrow hallway, use a lovely stripe carpet (7), which is a fantastic way of giving a neutral interior a subtle modern twist. Keep the fabrics simple and textured – contrast soft velvet (1) and fine corduroy (11) with wonderful new paper fabrics (3 and 5). Tone-on-tone patterns create a soothing, serene but interesting scheme – try linens or cottons in a simple gingham check (9), which is great for lining curtains, or an abstract pattern (4), and add richer luxurious textures with chic cashmere pinstripe (12) or silk with an embroidered motif (8).

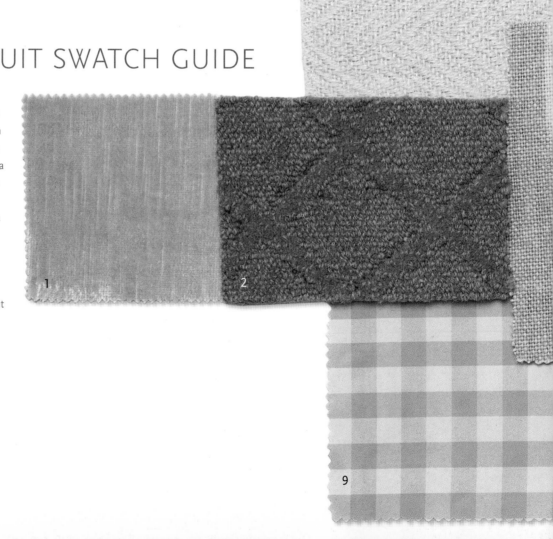

Another view of the living room on page 25, here showing more of the touches that, when added to these creamy off-whites, make for a rich decorating palette. This is not the uniform beige of yesteryear – this is contemporary but very comfortable, chic and grown-up but eminently liveable. Note the simple seagrass panels framed in cherry wood on the wall that faces the elaborate feathered headdresses. This juxtaposition, together with the abundance of varying shades and textures – the pale turquoise and moss-green cushions, the brown faux-alligator chairs, the seagrass chairs and the ottomans, which have a woven mahogany base and linen top – all create a perfect sense of balance in the room.

This comfortable off-white living room has been warmed up with earth tones. The walls, curtains, blinds and chairs, upholstered in oatmeal linen, form the cool basis of the scheme. This is given warm touches by the comfortable camel settee in a rich mellow wool fabric called 'billiard cloth' and chairs in mushroom-coloured polished wool. Accents are provided by the Chinese elm-wood table and ethnic African masks and bowls.

CALICO

STRING

LINEN

TWINE

OATMEAL

OATMEAL
TO TWINE

ALMOND

It is when one moves on to the oatmeal, string and stone colours that the picture changes slightly. I don't mean that these shades are not neutral enough to work with the other shades of off-white, but that their slightly ash-grey tone makes them feel less warm and more urban. These colours suit a more structured, tailored look and work well as upholstery. They also provide a perfect base for a room furnished with distressed Provençal or Gustavian pieces.

STONE

Cool urban chic

THESE SHADES ARE ON THE cusp of the light grey colours and are almost the direct opposite of the warm buttery tones of off-white. They are cooler in every sense of the word – in the hip sense and also in terms of the atmosphere they create.

Elegant, chic and a little bit edgy, this is the classic palette for urban loft spaces, which are often done out in shades of oatmeal, linen, string and stone. This is a grown-up, masculine style for the twenty-first century and is ideal for spacious open-plan spaces, as the colours and textures need room to breathe.

The light and dark shades look great mixed together in a tweed and used to upholster a modern sofa. Neat rows of suede and leather cushions in similar and milkier shades can be added to soften the effect yet remain in keeping with the smart tailored style that announces – 'I have arrived'. Window treatments need to be kept minimal – simple fabric screens or wooden shutters are preferable to fussy drapes or blinds.

ABOVE Decorator Frédéric Méchiche has performed a masterstroke by flanking a very graphic piece of modern art with a pair of long slim antique mirrors. As well as making the room wonderfully elegant, this combination provides a very neutral backdrop, which is perfect for the display of an eclectic collection of furniture. The room has a lovely feeling of balance and symmetry, in which the stone pillar and putty-coloured wall are softened by the mushroom velvet sofa and natural-fibre floor.

ABOVE This warm unstrident room is all about soft colour and texture. The main feature is the bed, with its interesting version of the padded headboard that is emerging as the bed accessory of the decade, here with vertical panels and a comfortable turnaround at the sides. Together with the different textures of the covers on the bed, it adds a tactile quality to the string and cappuccino-froth colour scheme.

OPPOSITE Oatmeal gives warmth to an otherwise often timid colour range and its nubbly finish makes it practical as well as beautiful. In Bernie de le Cuona's delightful living room the comfortable settees are accompanied by slipper chairs that have not only cushions but also carefully folded throws in accent colours, which can be changed to create a totally new look. The coffee table is an antique bed from West Africa – real wood always adds stability to a room.

On the floor, carpets and rugs in darker tones of these colours help to ground the scheme and add another layer of texture and tone.

For best effect, these shades benefit from textures of any sort, both rough and soft. Tweed and oatmeal are obvious choices for soft furnishings, but chenille, wool, wicker, stone, metal and wood will also show off these tones to best advantage. In fact, any material with feel and depth seems to enhance the smart look, whereas flat colour can look a little dull and dreary.

As these are the coolest shades in the off-white palette, they will benefit the most from warm accents in all the coffee shades – from latte and cappuccino through mocha to espresso.

LEFT This large outside living space in South Africa, designed by Stephen Falcke, is furnished with furniture by Dedon, a new company making wonderful plastic-coated designs that can be used and kept outside – practical as well as beautiful. The verdant garden setting forms a lovely backdrop for this pleasing room, with its collection of African bowls and accessories that bring a variety of tones and textures into the space.

ABOVE This light-filled room has sliding doors along two walls that open onto the outdoor living area. Similar colours and textures mean the spaces flow seamlessly into each other. The 'Louise' chair from Indonesia is displayed like a sculpture.

ANIMAL PRINTS
AS ACCENTS

■ Almost every designer I have spoken to recently has mentioned animal prints – especially the big cats. So it would seem that tiger, leopard and zebra prints have become a totally neutral accent – as cushions, throws, floor rugs or accessories in virtually every spectrum of colour one can imagine. The camouflage effect that these animals' skins have in their natural habitat is what makes these faux skins blend so well in home furnishing. It is hard to think of a colour that would not benefit from something in an animal print – the off-whites all love them.

When working with a subtle colour spectrum such as this, it can be very effective to add an unexpected touch, to make the whole room revolve around something interesting and different, something that no one would expect to find in such a gentle room. A metal sculpture, for example, or an unusual piece of furniture, a piece of heavy driftwood or an ethnic artefact – something that lifts the whole weight and texture of the room and makes it truly yours. Do remember, however, that although the ultra-minimal look is out, too much clutter is not the way to go and sometimes what is needed in finishing a room is to edit out rather than to add. Having said that, what is important is that the house is truly 'you' – featuring what you love and need to feel at home.

My conclusion about these creamy off-white colours in general is that the first group – the snow-white milky tones – are by far the easiest to use, as mistakes are virtually impossible. What is exciting, however, is to use these shades in interesting new ways and to add tones from the other butter to biscuit or oatmeal to twine groups for weight, texture, warmth and urban chic in the ways suggested above. In my view, a room in which shades from all three groups are used together may be more complex to achieve but the rewards are high – the effect can be magical.

ABOVE A traditional, elegant room is brought to the forefront of twenty-first-century decorating by the addition of a zebra-skin rug and a leopard-skin throw. It's details like this that can update a room and give it a *frisson* of excitement. There are many convincing quality prints available that are a good alternative to using the skins themselves.

LEFT In this house the sauna and gym lead into this wellness or relaxation area – a place to chill after a workout. Comfortable chairs and sofas are perfect for lounging and relaxing on and the cross-cut travertine floor looks wonderful covered with a simple Afghan rug. I love the use of real floors of this sort, as they seem to add an organic aspect to the design and space. The dramatic Mexican mirror is a pivotal decorative feature in an otherwise calm and peaceful room.

As curtains become simpler and simpler, it seems to have become necessary to add the ubiquitous sheer linen blind, in shades of white, to every window. These provide privacy and allow soft, diffuse light to pass through.

When using the greyer tones of off-white, you can introduce darker greys as well as earthy tones to ground the look. A dark grey-brown stone floor (10) can look very smart, while a glossy polished wood floor in a similarly rich colour (6) will give a warmer feel to an interior. If you prefer something soft underfoot, try a nubbly wool carpet (8) or a natural-fibre flooring such as sisal, coir or seagrass with an off-white border (7) to tie the scheme together. When layering fabrics, use a variety of fabrics in heavier and lighter weights. Fine linen weaves in stone or pale slate (2 and 4),

a large sand-coloured check (9) and the lightest cashmere (5) are ideal for window treatments, while the gingham and cashmere could also be used for cushion covers. A wonderful versatile oatmeal linen (11) is my fabric of choice for upholstery and is perfect used in large quantities in a scheme such as this. Touches of paper fabric (13) add another subtle texture, while small quantities of a sumptuous cocoa-coloured pattern (1) will step up the comfort factor, especially in winter. Hound's-tooth check (3) and a smart stripe (12) introduce a heavier weave and are very chic.

Accenting off-whites

ALL THE OFF-WHITE AND CREAM colours can be accented in many ways, but what is interesting is how they can be teamed rather than accented with the coffee and chocolate colours as well as all the ginger and cinnamon tones. Perhaps the rule should be that if it's a colour that sounds as though you could eat it, it'll work well with all other such edible colours: think coffee and cream; cinnamon and meringue; mocha and biscuit – all are perfect in layers and swathes. These, however, are not so much accents as an extension of one perfectly neutral range into another. All the off-white shades can be used with all the earth and spice colours without exception – the coffee and chocolate shades are obvious but sure-fire winners; the spicier colours require some caution but can create real zing.

| Ginger | Chocolate Pudding | Cocoa |
| Jade | Heather | Burnt Orange |

CREAM, HEATHER & CHOCOLATE

Bernie de le Cuona uses shades of heather, coffee, chocolate and cream to accent her oatmeal drawing room in a gentle and relaxed way. The rich wood table is an ideal setting for a mauve campanula – an unusually good choice of flower accent. The signature use of matching cushions and neatly folded throws forming a central stripe on the slipper chairs, each with a lamp angled over it, is a great look and is an easy, practical way to provide a colour accent.

MILK, SEAL & CHARCOAL

In an ultra-masculine magnificent riverside penthouse, Luigi Esposito has made a great vignette with these antique Italian chairs and a chinchilla throw. Adding vintage features to a room gives an indefinable 'wow' factor.

STRING, GINGER & COCOA

Vicente Wolf has cleverly used a twentieth-century table made from two different woods in contrasting tones as a focal point in this corner, introducing the two main accent colours. The dark brown is echoed by the African sculpture and the cushion, while the paler tone is reflected by the ginger leather chair.

STONE & GRANITE

Many different layers of texture have been introduced throughout this stone-coloured room. The only dark accents are added by the two large plinths, chair frame, lamps and cushion.

OATMEAL, PURPLE & COCOA

Dark purple and chocolate velvet cushions on oatmeal tweed add a richness and warmth to an otherwise fairly cool colour. It is important to note how changing accessories can completely alter the look and warmth of a room.

BUTTER & JADE

The soft green of the oil painting was the inspiration for the accents in this tranquil cream dining room accessorized by Katharine Pooley. The underplates are made of jade and the cutlery handles are a similar shade of shagreen. It's a good idea to start with an existing object or colour and keep within that colour range, but changing the texture whenever possible.

STRING & ACID GREEN
A pale string-coloured sofa and a steel and glass table add to the sense of airiness in this Parisian pied-à-terre, stunningly accented with acid-green glass – the colour of the moment in Paris and utterly chic.

CREAM & PALE TURQUOISE
A selection of magnificent velvet and hand-printed silk cushions in shades of soft greenish turquoise add immense glamour, texture and excitement to this off-white room. The patterns are replicated from original Louis XIV fabric from the Palace of Versailles and made exclusively for Katharine Pooley by Richard Fischer.

STRING, GREY & EBONY
The broad-stripe cushions, in pale grey and off-white with a fine ebony stripe, give the string-coloured sofa in this living room a twenty-first-century look – it's unstructured easy living, yet functional and smart. The textured sisal rug throws the angular dark lacquer side table into relief. The off-white throw over the arm is both practical and stylish.

GREYS • Silver Sea Foam Oyster Venetian Marble Pearl Ice Cube Mist Driftwood Brushed Aluminium Grey Flannel Abalone Seal Pewter Elephant Shadow Storm Cloud Granite Anthracite Charcoal Slate Ebony Grisaille Moonshine Cobblestone Silver Fox Dormouse Cement Pigeon Rhinoceros Zinc Wolf Steel Thunder Smoke Twilight Bunny Grey Mink White Water Anchor Cashmere Looking Glass Dolphin Rainfall Atlantic Ocean Donkey Pebble

Grey of all shades – from the very pale, softest cashmere and silvery greys to the dark moody slates and ebonies – has been a long time arriving in the world of home design. In the past it has always been thought of as edgy and very urban, and only to be used with caution. But suddenly grey has become an indispensable perfect neutral that is very versatile – in all its many tonal guises.

The warm, almost donkey-coloured grey used in this living room has a lush comfort factor built into it. The room is given a sense of excitement by Vicente Wolf's eclectic choice of furniture, especially the rough-hewn wooden side table and the magnificent carved hand silhouetted against the window. These two items throw this elegant room into perfect relief.

SILVER

ICE CUBE

Rather like an Armani suit, this elegant pale grey bedroom is all uncluttered lines and superb quality. Nancy Braithwaite has decorated it entirely in shades of soft grey, with no other colour introduced; the only pattern is on the bed cover and pillows – and that's also monochrome. Simple softly pleated Roman blinds beneath the heavy long curtains create a feeling of understated luxury. No item is out of place.

VENETIAN MARBLE

OYSTER

SILVER TO MIST

PEARL

SEA FOAM

MIST

The very pale silvery greys are perfect for a cool, elegant urban room. These are sophisticated, ethereal colours that are often accented with silver – the colour and metal of the decade – either through accessories or in the form of paint finishes, wallpaper or fabric. As soon as a hint of beige creeps into a grey, a much warmer look is achieved, and these shades can work equally well in a contemporary and more traditional interior setting.

Glowing grey

THE PALEST SHADES OF GREY seem to shimmer and glow with light, and even more so when combined with light-reflecting surfaces such as mirror, crystal, glass and silver. As a decorative tool, silver is being used increasingly in interiors to add instant glamour, to bring life to soft colours and to accent darker tones. Silver effects used to entail the painstaking application of silver leaf, but new technology has brought affordable alternatives in the form of metallic paints and wallpapers in many finishes and designs. Silver now glints and gleams in contemporary as well as traditional homes, in very different ways – sparkling and accenting, as well as forming a major part of a room – as a feature wall, room divider or piece of furniture.

One of the most pleasing and easy-to-live-with looks is undoubtedly the adaptation of the Gustavian style as seen in southern Europe and all over America. The pale grey weathered-looking painted furniture has evolved as a mélange of the Swedish and French Provençal styles. It varies interestingly from country to country and designer to designer, but wherever it is found it works well to create both stylish urban and relaxed yet stunning country looks. The elegance and neutrality of this 'weathered' grey-painted furniture is amazing; it's subtle and usable in almost any room of any house.

OPPOSITE The ornamental mirror, cornice and fireplace have been picked out in silver leaf, while the walls are painted in Not Totally White by French company Ressource. Michael Coorengel and Jean-Pierre Calvagrac have introduced a nineteenth-century crystal chandelier, a huge cowhide, a pair of 1927 Wassily chairs by Marcel Breuer, a 1970s Perspex table with granite top and a mirrored ball from a flea market.

ABOVE This is a perfect Scandinavian combination of white and grey. The arrangement of china on the shelves and the positioning of the sofa create an authentic symmetry.

LEFT A large silver mirror against a grey wall is juxtaposed successfully with a silver and steel table and a glass lamp.

With this pale grey washed-out furniture as the basis of a room, the decorating choices are myriad – one can go almost any way, from echoing the soft greys in various shades to adding bright accents or layering soft filmy fabrics, such as white linen for a bedroom. Pale grey is also marvellous with indigo Provençal prints and with fuchsia accents – in fact, there's nothing it is not good with, so the choice is yours.

There is something very English and 'classy' about pearl grey. It is understated yet very effective, but it does require a certain element of care, consideration and calculation to get the best result. Firstly, for walls, a balance of just enough – a mere dash – of beige needs to be added to pure pearl grey to take away all sense of chill; this is where experience and great colour sense are needed. Getting expert advice will pay dividends, as the difference between the right and wrong colour can be minuscule but huge in effect. Paint a large sample patch and consider its effect in all light conditions.

ABOVE Three square zinc vases by Christian Tortu have been used to add another shade of grey in a new texture to this living area, in which various shades of grey have been cleverly layered one upon another for a chic neutral effect.

LEFT The textured grey walls in this living area designed by Frank Faulkner are unpainted plaster. The junk shop chairs are unified with off-white loose covers.

OPPOSITE This glamorous bedroom-cum-seating area has been decorated by Sonja and John Caproni in soothing tones of pale grey and cream, with accents of darker grey in the form of a generously padded bed and sofa. The striking table base is a wonderful reconstituted stone tassel.

Once achieved, it is a subtle, warm, perfectly neutral look, without being remotely drab. Drapes in a shade a tad darker than the walls will add depth to the room.

Touches, or even swathes, of pearl grey work well in a bedroom, as it's such a mellow, evening colour. My creamy bedroom in London has almost by accident developed a grey touch, which seems to be increasing. It started with a Venetian painted four-poster bed in a distressed, almost 'dirty' colour, with flecks of gold leaf. This led to soft grey monograms on my pillows and bed linen. The soft greys have added elegance to the palette without reducing the warmth of the creamy tones.

LEFT This lovely shade of donkey grey provides a touch of warmth in this fabulously comfortable bedroom. The only two accent colours are the pure white bed linen and the hortensia that have dried to a stunning ginger. Vicente Wolf's signatures are all there: sheer linen blinds, very simple pure silk curtains that drop to the floor and extra-comfortable beds with padded backs and bottoms.

ABOVE The walls of this spare but cool Parisian room have been painted in chic pale grey, with a similar shade rug softening the mellow floor. Sheer drapes in a pearl grey dress the windows and the chairs are cream with grey cushions.

RIGHT AND BELOW

In the über-hip G Hotel in Galway, Ireland, Philip Treacy, best known for his dramatic hats, has designed this cool silver-grey double-height Grand Salon as a complete contrast to the shocking-pink one (see page 124). He has painted the French chairs silver and upholstered them in a silvery grey fabric that makes this the ultimate cool room, enhanced by the white carpet and ice-grey walls. The Perspex tables are filled with thousands of Swarovski crystals that catch the light; the metal sunburst mirrors by David Gill and a dramatic cluster of Tom Dixon's mirrored balls are marvellous touches.

ACCESSORIZING GREY TOP TIPS

■ Faded fabrics that have been printed to look as if they have aged are an ideal choice for a pale grey colour scheme. Companies such as Bennison Fabrics, Cabbages & Roses, and Chelsea Textiles, to name a few, produce this look in many designs from toiles to florals.

■ Silver creates definition in a room when it is used as an edging for furniture, mirrors or picture frames, or it can be teamed with another colour to form a glamorous wall covering.

■ Antique silver candlesticks have always been a traditional standby, used to bring elegance to a dining table. Today's manufacturers have come up with inexpensive yet stunning silver-plate versions of candlesticks, candelabra, vases and containers in many shapes and sizes, and these can be used to enhance a light grey scheme in many creative ways.

SILVER TO MIST SWATCH GUIDE

The most important point here is that because this is the palest palette in the grey colour spectrum, everything needs to go with pale stripped-down flooring – the best base for these colours. The ideal choice is textural bleached wood (3), off-white limestone (10) or, for a warmer feel, a natural fine wool carpet (4). Fabrics should be kept light and feminine, in keeping with the ethereal mood – shiny silks (1) and silvery velvety textures (5) that catch and reflect the light, soft tone-on-tone patterns (2, 8 and 14) or delicately embroidered fabric (12) could all be used for window treatments or upholstery. Textural pleated silk (9) would be ideal for large cushions or for simple Roman blinds, while transparent silk gauze with little mirrored sequins or crystals (6 and 7) would make pretty sparkling cushions, curtains or light-reflecting cloths to throw over tables or the back of a sofa. A soft boiled wool (11) adds a touch of warmth, while shagreen paper (13) brings a wonderful rich texture to walls.

ABALONE

SEAL

BRUSHED ALUMINIUM

Taupe velvet has been used on the back wall of this stunning bedroom designed by Luigi Esposito and accessorized by Katharine Pooley. The day bed and ottoman are covered in Alcantara (faux-suede) fabric. A fur throw on the bed gives warmth and luxury. Wenge side tables add rich colour, while the orange cashmere cushions, orange tweed cushions and throw, and orange flowers are the ideal accent for this exciting room.

DRIFTWOOD

DRIFTWOOD TO ELEPHANT

GREY FLANNEL

PEWTER

ELEPHANT

These mid-grey colours include the smarter tones of flannel and pewter as well as the softer, muddier shades that are on the cusp of the coffee and mocha colours – donkey, dormouse and elephant grey, for example. This is where grey meets brown, giving softer and less sharp-edged colours – perhaps for a warmer and less adventurous look. In this spectrum the dark and light tones used together are very subtle and calm.

RIGHT A grey dining area, with metal, glass and white leather furniture, is seen through one of the stunning acid green 'banisters' in this Parisian apartment (see pages 70–1). These were made from coloured plastic sandwiched between two glass sheets.

BELOW RIGHT Polished nickel Ralph Lauren chairs are covered in black-and-white tweed – a twenty-first-century twist on chic 1930s style. The charcoal carpet with black leather border adds another texture; the white chiffon voile curtains provide a total contrast, adding a lightness that is unusual and effective.

OPPOSITE In this bedroom designed by Luigi Esposito, a black leather bed dressed simply in black and white sits well against a bone faux-suede wall. The leather chair and rosewood table add weight to the room. The twill-covered ottoman is another example of suiting used as upholstery.

The warmer shades of grey

THIS SPECTRUM OF MID-GREY shades produces a warmer effect than the paler silvery hues and the moody, more masculine slate and granite tones. These driftwood to elephant colours have a touch of beige or taupe in them, which can change the tonality and increase the warmth factor instantaneously. As a result, these greys mix well with warm earth colours, such as bone, mushroom and all shades of brown. Such colours are a popular choice for bedrooms, as they're sophisticated and chic but also appealingly cosy. The taupe undertones are soothing and lend themselves to tactile luxurious textures such as faux fur, cashmere, silk and suede.

The crossover between fashion and interior design has become increasingly evident in recent years, with more and more names from the world of fashion now branching into home décor and producing their own ranges of home furnishings and accessories. Grey flannel – always a colour associated with understated elegance and a certain city chic for both men and women – is a case in point. This soft light to mid grey has successfully made the journey from smart fashion perennial to twenty-first-century lifestyle colour.

These flannel and soft pewter colours have an undeniable touch of Ralph Lauren-style to them, an understated elegance – in both clothing and home style. What I find most exciting, and liberating, is the way that these colours, when used in the home, can be layered, softened and accented in the same way as clothing. The amazing and different effects one can achieve are never-ending as well as beautiful.

As men's suiting has entered the curtaining and upholstery fabric world, with companies such as Ralph Lauren, Andrew Martin and Kelly Hoppen advocating the look, so a new and very masculine elegance has appeared. The stronger tones of mid grey are teamed with soft black leather and stainless steel, chrome or silver for a modern, manly room. Straight off Wall Street, these grey fabrics may have chalk stripes, a herringbone pattern, or windowpane, hound's-tooth or Prince of Wales checks. These very names conjure up a no-nonsense business-like feel, and personally I prefer the softer, warmer shades of grey – driftwood,

TOP LEFT A soft neutral bedroom in the G Hotel features an extra-wide padded bed back. With the walls, bed, sofa and curtains all in subtle shades of grey, the only colour in the room comes from the yellow hat in the picture, the white and marmalade on the cushion and the patterned stool.

LEFT This period dining room is painted in Sung Grey Mauve by Ressource, with the wood detailing picked out in crisp white. This, with the mellow old floor, provides a neutral backdrop for the superb mix of contemporary and antique furniture and accessories, in particular the graphic Arts and Crafts chairs by Charles Rennie Macintosh.

OPPOSITE The living area of Gérard Faivre's Paris apartment is painted in three shades of grey, the most dominant being Gris from Farrow & Ball. The large skylight roof allows maximum light into the room and makes it seem more spacious. The Bordeaux rug adds warmth, as do all the many interesting objects that make a room really liveable. The furniture is steel and white and elegantly simple.

RIGHT Here's how to furnish a room with great bed linen – a Ralph Lauren collection of safari colours, with a faux zebra-skin bed cover lined in velvet. It's not too 'matching' but goes so well as an ensemble. For the summer months it would be very easy to change the look of the room completely by using a lighter combination of bedclothes.

SAY IT WITH **FLOWERS**

■ Don't ever forget flowers as a decorative tool – one that can be added and altered without great expense or upheaval. Switching the flowers in a grey colour scheme from white roses to bright pink peonies changes the look of the room in an instant.

■ Vanessa Nahas, owner of Ma Maison on Fulham Road in London, recommends giving an elegant grey room a touch of colour by adding large bowls of flowers – the simplest and most economic accent in the world of decorating. She uses bold orange flowers in the winter and white or pale green in the summer. Blue and white Chinese jars and pots make pleasing vessels.

donkey, dormouse and elephant – which seem more versatile, contemporary and unisex. They can be used in masculine environments but also provide a soothing respite for those who live and work in a busy city.

As grey is a true neutral, the choice of accent colours is endless: with grey, almost anything goes. And for those who consider grey a dull colour and are surprised by its appearance in interiors magazines in the UK and all over Europe, let me suggest teaming these wonderfully neutral mid greys with acid green or yellow. The effect is instant sunshine and warmth, but in a different and very designer way, creating a new and unusual look. A dining room decorated in these colours, for example, accessorized with black-framed photographs or charcoal drawings, plus one of the new exciting stripes in grey, black and acid yellow – preferably in silk – and the result is 'wow'.

DRIFTWOOD TO ELEPHANT SWATCH GUIDE

This mid-grey palette can be used to create a smart, urban and quite masculine look, by using a mixture of men's suiting fabrics and leathers, as well as other textures in various tones of mid grey. Flooring can be simple stone (5), grey wool carpet (10) or sisal (3 and 12). These days, sisal flooring is available in an amazingly wide selection of colours and patterns, and can be used to add wonderful texture to a room. A combination of four different men's suiting fabrics (1, 2, 6 and 14) can be used for curtains, upholstery or cushions. I'm very taken with oatmeal fabric, here with a fine slate stripe (17), which tends to temper dark colours without causing them to lose their impact. The tone-on-tone paisley (18) and cowhide print (9) would have a similar effect used in moderation. As well as soft boiled wool (11), velvet (13) and silk (7), which catches the light, there are wonderful new sheers around that are guaranteed to add a glamorous dimension to any room (15 and 16). No longer available only in shades of cream, flimsy fabrics in unexpectedly dark colours will make a strong impact. The black textured woven leather (8) underlines the masculine feel, while bold touches of red leather (4) would be a wonderful accent that would also highlight the fine red stripe in the Prince of Wales check (14).

Black velvet walls make a dramatic backdrop to the charcoal and mid greys used by Luigi Esposito in this penthouse bedroom. The painting shows the way. The sofa is in charcoal-grey faux suede and the cushions and throws in a linen windowpane fabric – a chic effect. Elegant lamps and mirrors, with touches of silver and glass, add light and luminosity to this dark room. This look is a masculine one, but very liveable.

SHADOW

ANTHRACITE

EBONY

CHARCOAL

SLATE

SHADOW
TO EBONY

STORM CLOUD

GRANITE

In the same way that light, weathered shades of many colours become perfect neutrals in their most faded state, the reverse happens with dark colours. The deeper and more intense the shade, the more perfectly neutral it becomes. Very dark greys are ultra-chic and make a magnificent backdrop for an urban setting. They can be used for walls, upholstery and window dressings in slightly varying shades and textures to create a dramatic scheme.

Living in the shadows

SHADES OF DARK MOODY GREY, from anthracite and slate to the darkest ebony, can bring an unexpected sense of glamour to interiors. Although perhaps not immediately an obvious choice for home décor, where the aim is usually to enhance a feeling of space and maximize natural light levels by using pale, receding colours and light-reflecting textures, dark, saturated greys can prove a surprisingly effective decorative tool.

Traditionally used in domestic settings in the form of flooring and surfaces – slate tiles and granite countertops in kitchens or bathrooms, for example – or for architectural features such as fireplaces, these colours are steadily creeping onto walls, furnishings and other surfaces and accessories in many different textures and shades. With this new move toward creating moody, glamorous bedrooms and living areas,

I find that I now favour warmer, 'kinder' materials for worktops and splashbacks than the once ubiquitous granite, which, though chic, does lack a certain warmth and mellowness.

Rich dark greys, such as anthracite, are wonderful go-with-everything neutrals that I find especially comforting in winter – though with these darker tones I think a cream or a stone partner is more attractive than white, as this can look too cold. These shades work particularly well in sumptuous wool fabrics, as well as some of the marvellous new synthetic materials that are being made at the high end of the market, which have a filmy lustre to them. Once again, checks and patterns and many different textures of wool layer well here.

When painting or covering the walls, a dark grey flannel colour – either in a rich matt paint finish such as Francesca's Paints' Coopers Creek, or actually using flannel or another similar suiting fabric – can be hugely successful and gives the room a masculine English

OPPOSITE In a chic riverside apartment in London, Luigi Esposito has used anthracite wool to cover the walls of this room and accented them with modern drawings simply framed in silver metal. The chaise has a black leather base, black twill upholstery and a black throw. The rug is black pony skin – totally neutral but truly masculine and elegant.

CENTRE In London's fashionable Soho Hotel, designer Kit Kemp has cleverly juxtaposed three dark grey fabrics, each with a different pattern. The chair and the cushions are a fairly predictable grey and cream stripe; the interior of the bed canopy is a darker, French-style mattress-ticking stripe; the canopy itself is a cream and dark-grey toile. All these are in contrast to the crisp white bed linen and French quilt. This is a perfect way to use one colour combination that is chic and interesting but still fairly monochrome and neutral.

BELOW The rich tones and varying textures of the furniture and accessories in this room, designed by Coorengel and Calvagrac, especially the opulent French mahogany bed, are warm and mellow against the grand matt-black backdrop.

RIGHT A dark grey seating area in James Gager and Richard Ferretti's New York apartment, designed in conjunction with Stephen Roberts, is given textural interest by the rustic stack of logs in the hearth and the contrasting 1930s Murano crystal chandelier, which provides a light accent.

BELOW RIGHT A successful dark grey scheme can be created by combining a pale grey or white backdrop with dark grey furnishings and accessories. Dark greys and leather dominate this chic masculine bedroom.

OPPOSITE Contemporary versions of antique chandeliers are now widely available – in black, white, red and silver. This Baccarat example, hanging over a Belgian bluestone table on a Saarinen base, with 1951 Roland Ranier armchairs, is the dramatic feature of this room, in which other touches of ebony are evident.

library look; if you use fabric on the walls, it looks good with dull brass tacking or similar as edging. If dark walls are too oppressive for you, go for a paler grey with a touch of beige to warm it up – Pearl Ashes by Fired Earth or Crown's RIBA Drawings Collection Palladian 14, for example – and introduce glamorous moody greys through upholstery, bed linen, chairs or lighting.

Everyone knows that black is neutral – the little black dress can be accented with any colour under the sun and for many people it is the perfect garment. The same can be said for black used in home decorating, but it is a colour that requires caution.

An exciting way to use black in the home is to embrace the masculine look fully and use men's suiting material – the hound's-tooth, Prince of Wales

HOW TO **MAKE GREY WORK**

■ Choose a 'dirty' paint colour with a touch of taupe to add warmth. The golden rule is: too grey and it is stark and cold; too beige and it becomes another colour. Pure pigment paints or limewash with a wonderful 'old' colour will give the best results; try Éléphant or Borde de Seine from French company Flamant.

■ For a warm, mellow look use woollen fabrics, paisley throws and textured wallpapers or fabric wall coverings.

■ For a masculine look use men's suiting fabrics with leather and chrome.

■ The right accent gives an essential lift. Chinese red brings out the best in dark grey – use African headdresses or pieces of coral, as well as cushions and throws. Zebra blends superbly in a black room.

and windowpane checks, for example. All of these are the very essence of chic in a neutral scheme, but at the same time they are practical and hard-wearing choices.

Today there are more materials to be found in black than ever before, in patterns and plains. Leather and suede, fake fur and velour all make a good base for a dark scheme and can be layered with checks, paisleys and other patterns in colours from this spectrum. If you introduce off-white and taupe into the layering, you can use almost any accent colour. Furnishing in leather is a great look, but if you can find an old piece – or at least a chair or sofa that looks old and that has been given a 'weathered', worn appearance – it will add a very different textural dimension. Baroque-style lacquered furniture is a stunning and contemporary way to introduce black into a room, as are the dramatic new black chandeliers.

If a more feminine look is what's required, softer colours can be used or added to a dark grey scheme. The room can soon be warmed with lighter shades of grey and tones of soft silver, pearl and mink in cashmere or glorious textured alpacas and wools; or try a toile or stripe in grey and cream. These will all give a feminine touch to a room without losing the chic, smart feel.

ABOVE This clean, well-balanced, almost severe room with its striking black furniture is made superbly chic with the addition of an unusual chandelier by Tommy Parzinger – designer Larry Laslo describes it as 'looking almost as if a space ship is landing'. It is often the inclusion of a dramatic piece of furniture or art that awakens an entire room.

LEFT Bernie de le Cuona regularly changes the look of her dining room by using different fabrics, such as this black embroidered linen runner (see also page 150). The napkins were made from what she calls 'mutt cloth' (hound's-tooth tweed). This is a great look for winter.

This curtain in my guest bedroom is made from formal dark grey flannel with a white check pattern and is trimmed with crystal beads all the way down one side – rather pretty.

SHADOW TO EBONY SWATCH GUIDE

For this ultimate masculine colour spectrum, the fabrics I have chosen are also indisputably masculine – black leather (10), men's suiting fabrics in hound's-tooth check (1) and fine chalk stripes (7), fine cashmere in grey (4) and black (5), together with nubbly tweed (2) and two sand and ebony stripes (14 and 16). As always, a mixture of tones, textures and fabric weights is essential to keep the look interesting, with a touch of tone-on-tone pattern (13) for extra variety. These fabrics could all be used for curtains, upholstery, bed covers or cushions. Fine white linen curtains or simple blinds (6) can be used alone or layered with another fabric. Flooring can be dark wood (9), warm elephant-grey carpet (12) or tweedy natural-fibre flooring (8). I think the addition of a pony-skin rug (11) would add glamour and an up-to-date touch. Reds and pinks in plain or patterned fabric (3, 15 and 17) make fantastic accent colours for this dramatic palette; they add a feminine touch, too, but should be used sparingly.

Accenting greys

Light Orange   Chinese Red   Acid Green

Oxblood   Black   Silver

DONKEY & ORANGE

It is so important to add the correct colours to illuminate grey and prevent it from looking drab. A vibrant shock of colour, such as the burnt orange introduced by the cushion and echoed by the desk accessories and flowers, can transform what would otherwise be an understated room. When mid brownish grey is accented in this way, it gives a warm, rich glow to a room, which is further highlighted by the warm tones of the wenge table. This is a sophisticated colour scheme that is more urban than country.

MISTY GREY & ACID GREEN

This has to be one of the most stunning ways of accenting a grey room, and possibly the most exciting yet simple staircase I have ever seen. The staircase is constructed in steel with sheets of glass that have been tinted acid green inside; these were made in Belgium and Paris respectively. Acid green is arguably the most exciting accent colour of the decade and works in every neutral spectrum, but use with caution. Gérard Faivre has used it for the staircase and two vases – any more and the impact would be lost. Remember, less is more.

GREY OF ALL SHADES is easy to accent with verve and excitement. It calls out for small dashes of colour – and here one can be really bold and dramatic and still be assured of delightful results. Bear in mind, though, that since grey is a smart, sophisticated colour, it will work best in combination with strong tones.

Some of my favourite shades to use with grey can be seen in the palette, opposite. Burnt orange, oxblood and, of course, black and silver all make exceptional partners for all shades of grey, while Chinese red is stunning with the darker tones. Acid green is a daring but very effective choice for a pale grey scheme, while other bold choices are turquoise, cyclamen and fuchsia, which give a modern feel. Paler greys also work well with heather and maize, softening the stronger colours.

ANTHRACITE & CHINESE RED

Chinese red is an almost perfect accent with any neutral colour, but it is particularly striking when used with dark anthracite grey, as can be seen in this room designed by James Gager, Richard Ferretti and Stephen Roberts. The glossy red vases by Georges Jouve are stunning against the dark grey mantelpiece, and the same colours are repeated in the rug. The 1970s French acrylic lamp and the acrylic and leather sofa demonstrate that clear Perspex, like silver, is a perfect foil for dark grey.

GREENS

GREENS • Celadon Celery Daiquiri Key Lime Pie Mint Granita Fennel Pistachio Lettuce Pea Soup Pear Guacamole Leaf Winter Sea Jade Green Tea Thyme Sage Fig Moss Olive Tobacco Shagreen Leek Cucumber Pernod Lime Sherbert Margarita Gooseberry Avocado Chicory Willow Chartreuse Meadow Apple Verdigris Rosemary Eucalyptus Artichoke Grass Eau de Nil Fern Khaki Orchard Creamed Spinach Emerald Forest Crème de Menthe

Consider the green spectrum – from the pale, creamy tone of celery, through the freshest leaf green to the deepest, muddiest tobacco – and it is evident that green is a colour that is in perfect harmony with every other. One only has to look in the garden or visit a flower show to see endless shades of green coexisting happily with myriads of coloured flowers: a perfect neutral in all its many shades and strengths.

For this master bedroom Jamie Drake has chosen a temperamental yellow-green tone for the shantung silk curtains and a slightly darker raw silk to upholster the headboard. The cowhide on the mid-century modern chair echoes the rich browns of the walnut-stained floor and nightstand; emerald velvet and apple-green silk cushions add punch.

Vicente Wolf has chosen Dorset Grey fabric for the upholstery in this welcoming seating area. This pure celadon shade is the dominant colour in a charming living room that's flooded with natural light. The scatter cushions are covered in soft toning shades of old jade and pale basil in a rough faille hand-loomed Indian cotton. This works well against the display of rustic shovels on the shelf behind.

MINT GRANITA

CELADON

KEY LIME PIE

FENNEL

DAIQUIRI

CELADON TO PISTACHIO

PISTACHIO

CELERY

What works in nature, however, does not necessarily work in the home – some shades of green can be unappealing in certain lights. I find the soothing tones of the celadon to pistachio palette the easiest to work with. It is almost impossible to make a decorating mistake, as these are soft, easy colours that work in every style of interior and in every environment. These are what I call the 'Zen' greens, as they are the most soothing shades.

'Zen' greens

THESE SOOTHING SHADES of palest green bring an undeniable sense of spirituality and peace into a room, creating an interior that is a true sanctuary from the outside world of strife and tension – something every home should provide. Because of this quality these shades work well in any style of interior and can be used to great effect in all rooms in the home, from relaxing living spaces or sleeping havens, to serene dining areas and bathrooms – the ultimate retreat.

It is interesting to note that these soft 'Zen' greens are also very new and stylish colours in the world of home décor. They are versatile shades that epitomize a cutting-edge look that can be used in many different ways and to suit many different lifestyles.

One of the most beautiful and effective ways to use these pale colours is to layer all the many subtly varying shades of celadon, celery, mint granita, key lime pie, fennel, pistachio and daiquiri – changing the texture a little for maximum effect. It is always best to consider the maxim that the more space you intend to cover, the lighter and more delicate the colour should be.

Start by painting your walls a pale and understated shade. Try something with just a hint of colour, such as Flamant's Thé Vert or Francesca's Paints' Neisha Crosland II Sage – the perfect backdrop.

With fitted carpets in vogue again, perhaps a soft fennel shade would fit the bill? Stripped and waxed floorboards or natural stone slabs would also work wonders with this colour scheme.

For curtains and blinds, consider stonewashed linens and fine sheers. Go for a colour that's just a tad more intense than the walls but with a great deal of texture to add accent. There are also many wonderful new fabrics with self-patterns – sometimes using three or more different shades of soft green.

TOP AND ABOVE A serenely neutral effect has been achieved in this bedroom by using an antique-finish paint effect, which gives the appearance of age. The canopy, bed curtain, pillows and bed cover of the eighteenth-century English bed are in hand-embroidered Scattered Flowers linen fabric by Chelsea Textiles. The canopy lining and the headboard are a pale green silk. I love armoires that have wire-covered doors, as one can pleat fabric behind them to soften the feel of a bedroom – again, the fabric is Scattered Flowers. A lavender accent is introduced in the form of a pale gingham check.

OPPOSITE Agnès Emery has filled the walls of her chic celadon dining room with an amazing collection of mirrors. Using mirrors inevitably adds lightness and a sense of space, but nothing could have prepared me for this disparate collection, which gives the room a dreamy underwater quality.

FAR LEFT Interior designer Jason Bell has used two similar paint colours for maximum subtlety when revamping this kitchen. The cabinets and trims are in a pale shade of celadon and the walls are in a marginally darker tone. The slight change is a clever touch in layering.

LEFT Ming-green granite and mosaic tiling in shades of green give this bathroom a coolly elegant look. The sink with its polished metal stand adds a 1930s twist.

CELADON TO PISTACHIO SWATCH GUIDE

Working within this colour scheme creates a very different look that is fresh and interesting. It is perfect for elegant, grown-up interiors. Flooring should be understated, such as fine wool carpet in a soft greenish beige (11) or simple cream tile (4). The pale celadon marble (6) is very grand and would make a wonderful top for a console table. Shagreen wallpaper (7) brings texture to the walls, while fabrics in different weights, textures and self-patterns (3 and 14) can be layered throughout a room. The fine off-white linen with a narrow self-stripe (2) is ideal for curtains or blinds, while the oatmeal linen (1) is perfect for upholstery. The paper fabric (13) offers a soft and easy way to use lime green, whereas the slightly more acid-green herringbone (10) is more adventurous and would look lovely with the silk check (8). The gorgeous leaf-patterned silk (12), used sparingly, adds a grown-up touch. In contrast, the ostrich (9) is very daring but would make great textural cushions. The large embroidered flower (5) would make a beautiful centre for a cushion or chair back.

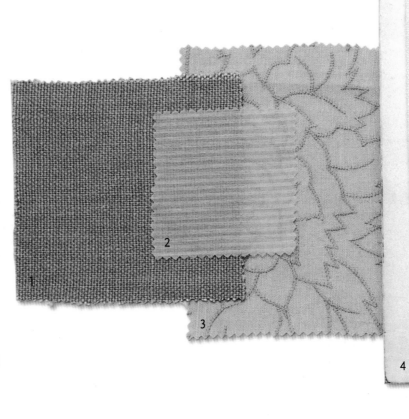

Once you have created a perfect 'Zen' environment, it is time to bring in more colour and depth and a little excitement. For upholstered furniture I love the idea of having one set of loose covers for summer and one for winter; it's such an easy way to alter the mood of a room. Perhaps a heavy linen in a darker shade of green than the walls and floor for summer and a dark sage plain or check for winter? A green patterned paisley or wool throw over the arm or back of a sofa gives instant warmth, while cushions in different shades of green can also add a different dimension.

This calm, quiet look is wonderful with Chinese furniture, as the dark wood is a perfect foil for the celadon colour scheme. Add an item or two in Chinese red as accent and the effect will be exciting yet at the same time peaceful and elegant. And finally, however contemporary your room, remember to add a vintage touch – it will serve to 'ground' your room perfectly.

JASON BELL'S TOP TIPS

■ Never try to match every element or piece of furniture in the same colour. Take your base colour and move up and down the various shades within that spectrum. Always remember the importance of texture.

■ Terracotta is my favourite accent for the celadon to pistachio spectrum.

■ Choose a style that suits you and your lifestyle. Buy a favourite interiors magazine for three months and mark every page you like. Look again after three months and a pattern of what you really like will emerge.

JADE

LETTUCE

The wonderful soft grey-green chenille that Jacquelynne Lanham has used throughout this stately dining room – for the walls as well as the curtains – seems to bring a dusk-like feel to the room, both day and night. The large gold-framed portrait, astrolabe and period furniture, together with the three crystal candlesticks on the bureau, give a late eighteenth-century air to this dining room.

LEAF

GUACAMOLE

LETTUCE TO JADE

PEA SOUP

PEAR

These are the classic greens – perfect neutrals where nothing jars, yet there is no feeling of lack of colour. There is a sense of both tranquillity and excitement in these shades – it all depends on how you use them. They can be effective as a base with exciting contrast colours, or used tone on tone and texture on texture for a peaceful, elegant room. These soft fresh greens also work well with a pale backdrop, or with dark wood and shades of brown.

WINTER SEA

Living with green and at one with nature

PERHAPS IT'S THE LINK with the natural world that makes green such an easy colour to live with. When we're surrounded by the stresses and strains of city living, a green colour scheme can help to restore the soul, providing a refreshing respite and letting us feel grounded and at one with nature. For country dwellers, a green interior provides a seamless connection with the outdoors and makes a fitting choice for a country kitchen with rustic wooden or painted furniture.

Personally I prefer the colour green for a living, dining or eating area rather than for a bedroom or a bathroom. Perhaps this opinion was formed because I grew up in an era when avocado bathroom suites were *de rigueur* and I still react rather badly to the thought of avocado green early in the morning or last thing at night. I was fascinated to be told by a leading Johannesburg interior designer that several avocado bathrooms he had removed from a house he was renovating had been purchased from him by a retro addict. So perhaps the avocado bathroom is coming back in vogue. In the meantime, while I remain unconvinced, chic bathrooms are appearing in the mellow neutral greens. Sea-foam green is a popular shade for surfaces in polished stone, or for painted or tiled walls, with towels in a darker shade layered with cream ones to give a revitalizing yet serene look.

Green is a perfect colour for living areas in almost all of its many shades. Elegant drawing rooms cry out for soft pear, perhaps with darker accents introduced in the upholstery, drapes and cushions. Lush grass and leaf shades are ideal in morning or garden rooms that open or look onto a garden, while cucumber or pea and cream make a lovely, fresh combination for kitchens. For a sophisticated dining area, shades of jade, shagreen and lettuce work well teamed with crystal and silver.

To prevent the stronger shades of green from overpowering, use a lighter tone as the backdrop and introduce the darker, brighter greens in small doses – as cushions, curtain tie-backs and tassels, trim on table linen and napkins, serving plates or glass vases. Strings of jade in green and yellow can be found in oriental bazaars and look beautiful heaped in glass bowls.

OPPOSITE A 'dirty' pear colour dominates one wall of this green bedroom, with its tranquil lavender accents. The walls are painted a paler green, but this darker shade is used for all the woodwork in the room, including the identical frames on the set of twelve French prints.

CENTRE A comfortable padded and buttoned bed back, innovatively made from a large gilded picture frame, adds texture and colour to this restful period-style bedroom in which the soft green wall is divided by the elegant pilasters.

ABOVE The shades of green used in this living room are moody and ever changing, so the atmosphere alters through the day. The armchairs are covered in a light sage ottoman textured fabric from Manuel Canovas. The upright chair is in cucumber chenille and the sofa is in a pale olive. The windows have off-white blinds and blue-green shades.

RIGHT The soft mid-green paint on the walls has been offset by the use of lots of milky white – on the ceiling, cornicing, louvred shutters, curtains and chair, as well as on some of the objects displayed on the table.

ABOVE FAR RIGHT Jacquelynne Lanham has effectively lifted this leaf-green wall with a display of light prints and cream antique plates.

RIGHT Coorengel and Calvagrac have designed this galley kitchen to be both immensely practical and really beautiful. The cabinets were lacquered black and given new heavy brass handles to create a vintage look. The winter-sea green paint on the wall – Chinese Turquoise by Ressource – is an elegant choice. Period objects mounted on the walls and optical views and maps inset into cupboard doors all add great personality to this fascinating kitchen.

MONA PERLHAGEN'S DECORATING TIPS

The owner and Creative Director of Chelsea Textiles has an exceptional understanding of colour and acknowledges how key it is to use the subtle 'off' colours to put together a professional-looking, liveable interior.

■ Keep the exciting, bright colour for accents and stay with the 'off' or 'dirty' colours as your base.

■ Chelsea Textiles fabrics are always in these soft, elegant and perfectly neutral shades. Available in many different patterns and combinations in each colour, they all have a wonderfully faded look that used to come only after generations of wear.

■ Simple checks and stripes, both large and small, are produced in each colour, so they can be used in combination with other patterns. In particular, use checks or stripes in toning colours to line curtains.

■ These subtle colours work beautifully with Swedish Gustavian furniture and weathered white-painted furniture, as well as with other types and colours of wood, such as mahogany, fruit wood, oak and pine.

With this green colour scheme as a base, you can accent and accessorize to create very different looks. For a more dramatic, less tranquil effect, add earth tones such as caramels and toffees, rich browns and rusty shades, as well as soft donkey grey. These colours will instantly make the room feel warm and autumnal rather than fresh and serene. This change is easy to achieve with the addition of throws and cushions in a variety of autumn-leaf colours. Introducing more pattern into the room will also create a warmer, cosier look. Consider, too, using a heavier curtain fabric.

For a more cutting-edge and contemporary look, add cool silver rather than warm wood tones and the fresh greens suddenly become very stylized and totally new. Furnish the space with metal, glass and Perspex pieces, silver accessories, mirrors and a modern artwork or sculpture, and this will achieve a very different look within this perfect neutral palette.

LETTUCE TO JADE SWATCH GUIDE

For schemes in this mid-green colour palette, flooring can either be warm honey-coloured wood (9), fine wool carpet in a soft fern green (13), cool pale limestone (7) or dark greyish green slate (8), depending on the effect you wish to achieve and the type of room you are decorating – carpet is more appealing in a bathroom, for example, while stone flooring is practical in bathrooms and kitchens. Soft textured woven fabric (5) or chenille (6) or cool pale stonewashed linen (1) are great for upholstery, while the gingham (3) is lovely to use for lining curtains. The embroidered motif (12) adds a touch of pattern, while the bold floral (4) incorporates a mixture of soft greens, blues and pinks; the subtle paisley (11) adds colour without making too much of a pattern statement. Both fabrics could be used for cushions, while the paisley would also be ideal for a throw. The snakeskin-effect leather (2), would make stylish cushions, as would the textured fine knit fabric (10).

SAGE

GREEN TEA

This soft shade of green – like creamed spinach, but actually a Williamsburg Collection paint, called 'Purdie House Gray' – is the perfect choice for the exquisitely simple country dining room of Pamela Kline's eighteenth-century Dutch farmhouse. This perfect neutral is a stunning foil for the rich earth-toned terracotta floor, antique baskets on the shelf, candelabra and period refectory table and Windsor chairs.

FIG

MOSS

GREEN TEA TO TOBACCO

THYME

OLIVE

TOBACCO

This colour palette is not for the faint of heart. These trendy dark greens are much more difficult to work with than their paler cousins, but when done successfully the results are striking and it is well worth the effort. Many fabric houses are now featuring these colours in wild and wonderful patterns and with great accent colours. As always, do try out paint colours and large returnable samples of fabric in situ before you buy.

Dark, meditative shades of green

FAR REMOVED FROM THE paler, fresh leafy shades of green, moody olive and smoky tobacco suggest a more masculine mood, conjuring up images of traditional libraries or gentleman's clubs. Yes these urbane colours can also be paired with bright accents such as turquoise or raspberry for a trendy young look.

Tobacco is a perfect example of one of the new and somewhat unexpected neutrals. It is a very fashionable colour that imparts a chic, smart look to a room and adds strength and interest. It is on the cusp of both the green and brown colour families, so it can be used to great effect layered with tones and textures from either palette. There are some wonderful paint colours: Fired Earth's Wild Olive and Flamant's Olive are strong dark tones; Beauvais Green and Pastis from Flamant are choice mid-colours; Francesca's Limewash in Maurizio's Cord is a pale shade that is ideal for walls. Among the fabric designers, F Schumacher and Brunschwig & Fils feature tobacco in their latest ranges – as a main colour and as a shade that works well with silver, acid green, turquoise and all sorts of other funky colours, as well as coral and terracotta for a more traditional look.

Olive green is rich and grand and looks wonderful in the new watered velvets. Artichoke is harder and less neutral. Forest shades all blend together and come in wild jungle patterns in mixes of greens with banana palms and huge leaves by Boussac and Brunschwig and many others. To create a wintery look, add mocha and ginger; for a more summery vibe, try tropical and palm prints – perfect mixed with creams and a hint of coral.

ABOVE LEFT The aged dark green paint provides the perfect backdrop for this room, designed by David Carter. The ancient Chinese sign blends with the eclectic furniture; the pair of silk lamps and the jade-green table add to the oriental mood.

ABOVE In this East Hampton home, Larry Laslo has created a cosy almost tobacco-brown guest bedroom that has a warm and welcoming feel. The addition of lovely crisp white linen with narrow red inlays is effective and smart.

OPPOSITE David Collins's appealing room is like a dish of olives, with all the different shades – on the curtains, carpet and chairs – mixed together. The embroidered stripe on the curtains lifts the dark olive silk and catches the light.

LEFT This den is a dark, cosy and intimate space that is perfect for relaxing in. The walls are dark khaki, while the sofa is a rich coffee-bean brown. With natural materials introduced through the woven table nest and flooring, and accents of leopard print and white, the room is as smooth and seductive as a piece of dark chocolate.

BELOW A bold shade of fig green has been used to define a shelved alcove behind a dining area. Painting a feature wall to denote a new zone in an open-plan space, or just for visual interest, is a great way to use stronger tones without them becoming overbearing. The table, designed by Terry Hunziker, is quarter-sawn white oak veneer and steel. The Russian birchwood chairs are nineteenth century.

IDEAS FOR PERFECT
NEUTRAL FLOORING

■ Gleaming polished wooden floors make a style statement: either stripped wood in mellow or dark colours, or painted white, distressed and then waxed.

■ Stone floors are wonderful and are a practical choice now that they can be warmed from beneath. Mellow golden stone glows, giving a new vitality to homes.

■ Stone cut into squares, then cemented and grouted, makes great outdoor/indoor floors.

■ Mottled bricks laid in chevron patterns can be waxed or left with a rough finish.

■ Travertine is a good alternative to stone flooring and is a richer creamy colour.

■ New sisal with double-edged borders is a modern substitute for carpet.

■ Animal-skin rugs – sheepskin, cowhide and zebra – work with all perfect neutrals. Alternatively, try oriental or striped runners.

GREEN TEA TO TOBACCO SWATCH GUIDE

A dark wooden floor (7) is the perfect choice for any room decorated in dark olive and tobacco colours. This is a difficult palette to work with, so you need to play around to make sure you've got the balance of colour, pattern and texture right. The wonderful no-colour chinchilla coconut fabric (5) is the perfect take-anywhere, use-anywhere shade and would be a useful addition to any scheme. The marvellous deep olive khaki (8) is dark and heavy, so is best used in small touches. The paper fabric (10), self-patterned fabrics (2 and 6) and the moss-coloured velvet (12) all provide great tone and texture, while the chartreuse in silk (14) and the toning stripe (9) is the colour of the decade. The bold leaf pattern (13) adds a lot of life and could be added to a room for a summery seasonal twist. The textural stripe (4) features a great combination of all the colours to help tie a scheme together. The fine white linen (11) works with every colour, while the two shades of check (1 and 3) are, as always, excellent for lining curtains or simply for cushions or upholstery. A spot-on combination of fabrics here would be: 4, 5, 10, 13 and 14.

Accenting greens

NATURE IN ALL ITS GLORY has shown us how many colours work well with the many various shades of green. What you choose will come down to personal taste and style, and the look you are aiming to create.

All shades in the green spectrum – light and dark – can be mixed with warm earthy colours such as rich brown, mocha and ginger for a cosy autumnal interior that exudes comfort and warmth. Luxe textures such as leather, velvet and fur work well in such schemes.

Brighter shades of red, orange and terracotta make eye-catching sunny accents for the darker palette, while zingy turquoise, fuchsia and peony pink will change the pace and give a cutting-edge look that will work particularly well in a more contemporary setting.

Shades of off-white and lavender combine especially well with the paler greens for a fresh but tranquil air.

Lavender **Piedmontese Aubergine** **Sun-dried Tomato**

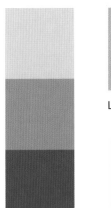

Gesso **Oriental Orange** **Mahogany Brown**

TOBACCO & TOMATO

In this eclectically furnished room in David Carter's house, the soft but vibrant red of a feathered tribal headdress from the Cameroons stands out beautifully against the dark tobacco panelled wall with its aged craquelure effect. The red is repeated in the rug design and on the drum table.

OLIVE & FUCHSIA

Before I had seen this unusual colour combination for myself, I would have thrown up my hands in horror at the idea of teaming olive with fuchsia. But it is actually a stroke of genius, as it brings life and a wonderful *joie de vivre* to these rich dark silk curtains.

CELADON & LAVENDER

Shades of lavender and violet are wonderful for accentlng green. The bed cover is hand-quilted in mauve Clematis fabric from Chelsea Textiles. The headboard and cushion are a cheery gingham check. Clematis fabric is also available in mauve but with a green vertical stripe. This version of the fabric is used for the curtains in this room (not shown here). Using such fabrics provides an easy way of getting two fabrics – and indeed two different colours – to work together.

BLUES
• Duck Egg Wedgwood Bluebell Light Teal Sky Aquamarine Denim Lilac Wisteria Lavender Forget-Me-Not Thistle Hyacinth Heather Violet Indigo Deep Teal Peacock Cobalt Blue Petrol Midnight Baby Blue Lapis Lazuli Mallard Sapphire Ocean Agapanthus Powder Blue Hydrangea Purple Crocus Amethyst Scandinavian Blue Caribbean Sea Blueberry Airforce Blue Cornflower Navy Lagoon Turquoise Lizianthus Spring Water Marina Gentian

Blue, as a colour in decorating, has really come into its own in the twenty-first century. No longer is it only the blue of Chinese porcelain teamed with white that is permissible; no longer are shades of pale blue the province of baby boys; no longer is turquoise too outré for words – all the blues from duck egg through lilac and teal to petrol are in fashion and are being used more and more by acclaimed designers.

Turquoise is not an easy colour to work with but here, in this inviting room, Jamie Drake has achieved harmony. Focus is provided by an amazing collection of antique Murano glass in opaline turquoise, displayed on a vintage table with other objects in similar shades. The colour statement in the room is generous, with curtains and throws in the same blue spectrum.

DUCK EGG

WEDGWOOD

The wall of this dining area, painted in Pale Medici Blue by Ressource, is bare apart from an ornate nineteenth-century Venetian mirror. The almost navy period settee is a perfect, if unusual, touch against the wall, as is the pale lavender undercloth. The dinner service is Voiles, designed by Michael Coorengel and Jean-Pierre Calvagrac for Puiforcat. The stunning 1940s chandelier, in three shades of copper, is by Jansen.

SKY

DENIM

DUCK EGG TO DENIM

AQUAMARINE

BLUEBELL

LIGHT TEAL

Blue, the colour of the sea and the sky, in all their many wonderful variations of tone and depth, is a supremely soothing colour to live with. But not all shades of blue are perfect neutrals – once again, it is the 'dirty', 'off' shades, the ones that look slightly aged and not too paintbox fresh, that provide the most successful backdrop for tranquil bedrooms and living rooms. The other stronger and more vibrant shades work well as accents.

Nature's paintbox comes indoors

THE MANY SHADES OF PALE and mid blue can be used to create wonderful effects all around the home – from elegant duck-egg living rooms and calming bluebell bedrooms to fresh aqua bathrooms and pretty Wedgwood-blue kitchens. These colours can be teamed with off-whites, greys and taupes, and accented with many shades from hot pink or yellow to silver or gold.

The palest, faded shades, such as duck-egg blue, powder blue and baby blue, are soft, gentle, dreamy colours that look heavenly on textural limewashed walls – reminiscent of rain-washed summer skies – as billowing linen curtains, in shimmering washed silk or as cashmere and wool cushions and throws. Linen loose covers on chairs are great in these shades, too. In fact, as an all-over colour in almost any room, the palest shades of blue are pretty unbeatable. They can be layered with slightly deeper blues, always using the lightest colour for the largest expanse of the room. They can also be layered with different fabrics and textures.

Aquamarine, the colour of clear mountain pools under a cloudless sky, is a younger, hippier relation with a touch more attitude – more turquoise and more rock-chic. All the same things apply as above but the result is younger and slightly brasher – more fun, perhaps. Surprising colours for a perfect neutral, the glorious shades of summer skies and swimming pools look astonishingly good together, as well as providing vibrant accents in a calmer scheme of gentler blue tones. With a little iridescence – try silk, glass or pearlescent tile – these shades become the magical elements of a blue scheme.

The Egyptian collection at the Louvre in Paris glows with turquoise and lapis – colours as old as time. The ancient Egyptians, and other early cultures, used these shades of blue with reverence and for their most prized objects.

Denim, a staple in most people's lives the world over, is not just part of everyone's wardrobe – it has also entered the world of home style with a bang. This ubiquitous fabric is hard-wearing and easy to clean, making it ideal for much-used spaces – a teenager's room, for example. The casual-chic look works well at the seaside, but also creates a relaxed mood in town and country alike. The colour varies from washed-out pale to indigo, and all blues in between. As anyone who wears it knows, there is no colour that does not sit well with it – a perfect neutral both in colour and texture.

OPPOSITE LEFT The colours in Eldo Netto's river-view apartment in Manhattan were inspired by the sky and river, as seen from the apartment. A pale 'off' blue wall is highlighted by a deep teal eighteenth-century architectural façade and three sepia pictures with blue mounts. This is a subtle way to accent and emphasize the blueness of this beautiful room.

OPPOSITE RIGHT This multiple bench in duck-egg blue, designed by Martin Hulbert, is the outstanding feature of Colette's Lounge at the Grove Hotel in Hertfordshire, designed by Mary Fox Linton. The different textures of the duck-egg walls, upholstery and Jim Thompson silk cushions make this blue-on-blue scheme work so well.

LEFT A Venetian mirror is the item that brings together this pale blue bathroom designed by the legendary Alberto Pinto. The mirror makes everything look pearly and opalescent.

ABOVE An antique sofa has been upholstered in a fine pale blue silk with a magnificent sheen and this sets the tone for this gracious drawing room designed by Eldo Netto. The black japanned cabinet, dark diamonds on the contemporary rug and pink flowers all accent the blueness. The leopard-skin cushions add a sense of newness to this period room.

RIGHT Eldo Netto had these curtains made from two colours of silk taffeta, which were cut and joined to form wide stripes. The colours represent the hues of the sky and river that change with the light. The nineteenth-century striped carpet was made in Agra, India, a city famous for the blue shade in its durries.

BELOW RIGHT Cotton Blue paint by Ressource is accented by an abundance of gilt in Michael Coorengel and Jean-Pierre Calvagrac's period-style library. It's an electrifying look for a room filled with paintings and curios.

USING TURQUOISE

■ Katharine Pooley, owner of the home accessories emporium, suggests using different shades of turquoise to add sophistication and presence to a neutral scheme.

■ Layer silk velvets and printed silks in shades of turquoise with neutral linens for a soft, balanced atmosphere.

■ A touch of chocolate brown prevents strong contrast between the turquoise velvet and pale neutral shades of linen.

DUCK EGG TO DENIM SWATCH GUIDE

These gentle pale blue colours once made up the classic seaside palette, but these shades have recently become more sophisticated and are now often used to create a very chic urban look. Hard flooring should be pale bleached wood (5) or sand-coloured stone (7), while softer options include rough-textured natural-fibre

flooring (4) and lumpy clotted-cream wool carpet (9), which provides a touch of luxury underfoot. Together with the silk velvet (13), fine cashmere (1) and knitted fabric (6), this brings warmth and comfort to the room. Once again, plain linens in two different tones (14 and 15) are practical choices that can be used anywhere, while the

Ruffle Linen by de le Cuona (3) adds textural interest. A touch of pattern could be introduced by the subtle stripe (2), the muted paisley (8) or the delicate floral embroidered fabric (12). The two different coloured silk taffetas (10 and 11) are the fabrics that were made into wide-striped curtains by Eldo Netto (see opposite top).

This bedroom by Jamie Drake is a play on lilac from floor to ceiling. The oversized headboard is tufted velvet in a purple shade with modern buttoning. The mattress covers are also tufted velvet but in this case it is a herringbone. The paint colour, the lacquered bookcases and the curtains are all in the same shade of lilac. The cream bedspread and cushion, each with a hint of lilac, complete this perfectly wonderful room.

FORGET-ME-NOT

LILAC

HYACINTH

THISTLE

WISTERIA

LILAC TO HEATHER

LAVENDER

These are blues with a touch of pink, lilacy tones that in the darker shades become heathery and full of depth. They are very new colours to be adopted by decorators, but used correctly and with subtlety they can be quite stunning. As ever, the best shades are those that have been paled-down, dirtied and weathered, as this makes them sophisticated rather than sweet; stylish and never cloying – and far from dull.

HEATHER

Romantic tones for summer and winter

LILAC IS A COLOUR that in my opinion is best used in its palest form when decorating. It is wonderful used as a pale, almost watery colour on walls and on woodwork – perhaps even with a slight limewash finish to make it look used or old rather than spanking new. It is romantic and summery when used like this and provides a perfect neutral backdrop from which one can work with great ease.

Using lilac in its stronger, deeper tones is more complicated and needs the magic touch of someone like Jamie Drake, who uses this shade to great effect in both the bedroom and living area (see page 102 and opposite). My advice is to take great care when attempting to cover large spaces with a denser tone of lilac, remembering that any error could be quite catastrophic – it is so hard to gauge the effect of strong colour on the walls after having seen only a small sample.

In terms of fabrics, however, one can find a wide range of deep but soft shades in a variety of weights and textures. Patterns in these colours are also very rewarding to use – stripes in heavy linens, ginghams and paisleys that all blend and contrast well with the pale walls I am suggesting.

When one gets to the more heathery shades, it becomes so much easier, as heather is a slightly less clean and definite colour than its lilac cousin. It blends, tones and works with almost any colour under the sun, so it layers to perfection. This deep shade is good in stonewashed linen, cashmere and chenille – as well as many other textures. It can work in winter and in summer, and is as good in a bedroom as it is in a living area – it is also fabulous teamed with other

LEFT I love the colour of heather – a very English or perhaps Scottish colour. One of the few fabric manufacturers to achieve this special, subtle shade is Bernie de le Cuona's company. Here she has created a warm and most unusual bedroom, with a heather peasant-linen throw with stunning long suede fringe, an antique paisley woollen throw and taupe and berry suede cushions – a perfect winter look that can easily be transformed into a summer room by a change of pillows and covers. Using colours cleverly permits this versatility. Keep a pale cream base for the summer, then slip heather-coloured covers on the headboard and bed base and layer heather cushions, covers and throws on the bed.

OPPOSITE A stunning soft lilac room by Jamie Drake, given a twist by the use of a textural heather-mix fabric that is offset beautifully by the lilac silk cushions.

OPPOSITE In this hall Mona Perlhagen has used two fabrics in identical colours. The curtains are in a design called Thistle in heathery indigo on cream linen, printed and embroidered for a very luxurious effect. The chair and bolster cushion are embroidered only, giving a lighter look. The warm wood panelling and carpet, together with the fabulous Arts and Crafts-style fabrics, give a unique look.

ABOVE RIGHT By using the palest of thistle shades for the simple silk curtains and a slightly darker greyer shade for the chairs, this dining room in Deborah Brett's London home is given a very serene feel. Unusually, it is a dining room that can be used both day and night. The wrought-iron mirror and glass chandelier and candelabra add texture and glamour.

RIGHT Frédéric Méchiche has achieved a stylish look by painting the walls a neutral lilac with a touch of beige, which blends well with the natural-fibre rug on the dark wood floor. The nineteenth-century day bed is covered in a chic modern stripe.

paler shades of purplish or pinkish blue, such as lilac, lavender, wisteria and thistle. Heather seems to have taken on the mantel of last year's taupe and beige as the universal colour of neutrality.

A great advantage of decorating a room in shades from the lilac to heather colour spectrum is that there is a never-ending supply of beautiful cut flowers in these colours that can be found all year round for a calming tone-on-tone effect. In the spring I use simple, elegant tulips or wonderfully scented hyacinths, stocks or sweet peas, either two different shades in separate large bundles or mixed together for a more relaxed and informal look. Lilac and wisteria blooms come in early summer but they don't last very long. Then there are lizianthus and, of course, heather itself. I have also found that campanulas in a deep lilac shade look good planted in bowls.

If you want to use a contrast colour that is original but still mellow, I discovered through a window display by Bernie de le Cuona that maize yellow is a perfect if unexpected 'wow' with heather, whereas acid green is a better shade to use with pure lilac.

LILAC TO HEATHER

A harmonious blend of soft lilac and shades of true blue give Lena Proudlock's Scandinavian-style kitchen/dining room a sophisticated but relaxed mood. The woodwork, cupboards and tabletop are painted pale lilac to blend with the collection of blue and white china. The seats of the painted chairs are upholstered in toning denim fabric.

LILAC TO HEATHER SWATCH GUIDE

JAMIE DRAKE OF DRAKE DESIGN ASSOCIATES ON USING COLOUR

■ On the subject of colour, I am NEVER neutral! There are no grey areas and I'll never whitewash my opinions. Yes, we live in a crazy, noisy image-saturated world and we all want serene, tranquil nests to which to retreat. So minimalism was born, and colour was retired to the crayon box from which joyous expression came. And then we were left with white boxes that lacked only the padded walls to illustrate fully the neutral madness that had overtaken design.

■ What I find tranquil is nature; and where in nature do you find beige? Been in a taupe forest lately? Did your heart flutter when your lover sent you ecru roses? Years ago, my art professor referred to colour as 'the musical part of the painting'. I approach my interiors with a similar notion, and I want my environments to sing! One way to accomplish a colourful yet harmonious space is to use the same colour in varying textures and tones throughout – at the windows, on the walls, for upholstery – and then add one accent colour.

■ Colour, like life, is relative. A cobalt-blue felted pool table jumps and pops and screams in a white room. Paint the walls a shade of sky or robin's egg and it cools down the hysteria, takes away the heat of contrast and 'neutralizes' the space. A bedroom painted lavender with floor-to-ceiling lavender-lacquered built-ins and purple headboard reads as neutral because all the elements are at a similar level of intensity.

The lilac to heather palette can look very trendy and new when expressed through a plethora of stripes, checks, paisleys and tweeds, together with some plain stonewashed linens. It's a subtle, unfussy, sophisticated and serene look that works well in bedrooms and living rooms alike. The Chelsea Textiles check (16) is an expression of possibly the perfect neutral lilac colour – a wonderful 'dirty' shade. Flooring can be pale oak (8), buttery limestone (13) or off-white tweedy wool carpet (9). The 100 per cent cashmere fabric (12) is beautifully soft and is just the right shade to tone with the check, the irregular stripe (14), the paisley (6) and the beautiful de le Cuona heather linen-mix fabric (4). The lighter summery fabrics (1, 2 and 5) can be replaced or added to for a cosier look in winter, using the richer textures, heavier weights and darker colours (3, 10, 11 and 15). The stunning silk stripe (7), which introduces emerald green and teal to the palette, would add a very dramatic look to the room. It would be glorious as curtains.

Using throws in a mixture of textures and toning colours, both patterned and plain, is a quick, easy way to change the look of a room.

INDIGO

VIOLET

PEACOCK

The antique sofa that forms the main feature of the Blue Lounge at the Grove Hotel has been covered in a blue crushed velvet, which is juxtaposed with cobalt-blue urns from the South of France. The contrast between these blue items and the soft mushroom paintwork and dark wood floor is stunning, but at the same time neutral. Sculptural wrought-iron objects are being used more and more in modern decoration – and I like it.

COBALT BLUE

VIOLET TO MIDNIGHT

MIDNIGHT

DEEP TEAL

PETROL

M oody, dramatic, sexy and glamorous, these glorious purple-blue colours are true night-time shades, ideal for dining rooms, formal drawing rooms and dramatic boudoirs. These are the colours that summon up an image of a screen siren on Oscar night, her silk skirts swishing as she sashays down the red carpet. A room decorated in tones from this spectrum should be dressed with equal glamour, in shimmering silks, rich velvets and glowing glass.

Moody blues for night-time glamour

RICH, EXOTIC BLUES and purples such as violet, crocus and indigo are undergoing a renaissance in home décor. French and Italian lifestyle magazines are even calling indigo the new black – and that says it all.

Indigo is the colour of Africa, the Orient and Central and South America. It also reminds me of countries such as Greece, Spain and Morocco, where the sun is so strong that it tends to drain and bleach colour. So

vibrant shades of indigo are used to 'beef up' the look and feel of tiles and fabrics. These versatile deep blue shades make great bases and accents, and can be used in many tones and fabrics, for either ethnic or sophisticated looks; with these tones you can achieve almost any effect you desire.

With the African style in vogue, I looked to Morocco for the amazing deep blues found in ceramics and glass.

Often these pieces are accented with turquoise – which also appears as trim on white tablecloths. Heavy cobalt-blue glass is a truly effective accent for a blue scheme – stunning displayed in living rooms, in kitchens or on dining tables. With affordable Moroccan and Mexican glass and ceramics now widely available all over the world, these accessories are a great way to add instant depth of colour to an otherwise quite dull blue room.

At the other end of the spectrum is midnight blue. This glamorous evening colour is my favourite for night-time dining rooms. It is at its best with soft lighting, candles, gleaming silverware and white table linen. This is an elegant look that puts one in the perfect mood for an evening of fine food and wine. For less formal rooms midnight blue can be used as a background colour to contrast with almost any hue – peony pink and creamy whites; all the shades of pale to mid blues; not to mention acid green. Use it for barbecues and alfresco meals with patterned ceramic plates and Mexican glass.

OPPOSITE A regal room by Jamie Drake, who never puts a foot wrong in his use of colour. Shades of purple and violet create an evening room that is elegant, comfortable and exciting yet still quite neutral, as all the colours are shades of each other, with the walls being the palest tone.

CENTRE Stephen Falcke has used two toning shades of violet and lavender for these dining chairs: using only the darker colour might have been overkill but like this, the look is perfectly in balance. The fabric is Alcantara (faux suede) with chic brass buttoning. The colours work well with the Turkish rug – choosing a rug that blends with, rather than matches, the colours you are using makes for a sophisticated, unstudied décor. The antique kimono echoes these shades.

BELOW In the fabulous G Hotel in Galway, Ireland, Philip Treacy has bravely juxtaposed midnight-blue walls with violet upholstery: it shouldn't work well but it does. The outrageously rococo gilded mirror is the perfect touch, as are the gilded *boiserie* and amazing glass lamp.

Somewhere in between the glorious violets and indigos, the smart cobalts and sexy midnight shades, are the dark and moody greenish-blue tones – teal, peacock and petrol. Teal is hard to define, as no two people see it in the same way. To me, teal is a strong blue with an infusion of both green and turquoise to form a deep, resonant colour – often seen on mallards. Teal is a great new perfect neutral, as it can be used so successfully not only with other blues and greens but also with all the earth tones, especially coffee shades. This splendid colour is best in rich fabrics that let it glow; it can be used extensively in living areas and is also a fine accent colour – in the form of glass and china, in particular. As with all rich colours, use teal with caution and experiment with large returnable fabric samples to assess the impact of such a colour.

Another favourite shade is a strange mixture of dull turquoise with hints of Atlantic winter sea – I know no better way to describe it. It is a perfect neutral shade and can accent almost any colour – I love it with all the creams and coffees as well as greys, but recently saw it accenting an acid-yellow kitchen, and it saved the day.

ABOVE Indigo walls are a great choice for dining rooms, as so many are used principally at night. The gold candelabras are a perfect accent for this colour – as are crystal and silver. In fact, all the luxury materials look stunning with indigo.

LEFT This dining room in an early Victorian town house has been given an almost baroque feel by designer John Minshaw, who has chosen a deep indigo blue for the fireplace wall where the Elizabethan portrait is displayed, and complemented this with the paler blue chair covers and dark furniture.

DINING ROOM STYLE TIPS

■ In a dining room decorated in dark moody colours, use an abundance of glass and silver, as these will twinkle and sparkle when they catch the light, lifting the look and bringing the room to life.

■ Candlelight is a must; always use white or cream candles and remember to light them before your guests arrive.

■ Use flowers either in the same colour as the room for a tonal effect, or to add a colour accent – for example, imperial-yellow flowers look wonderful with blue; bright pink complements any colour.

■ Alternate glass candlesticks with small bud vases all the way along a table, as they look pretty and won't obscure the view of the person opposite.

■ Instead of buying tablecloths and mats, use a central runner and underplates; make napkins out of unexpected fabrics.

VIOLET TO MIDNIGHT SWATCH GUIDE

With such a dramatic dark palette, flooring can either blend in tones of moody blue stone (5) or create a bold contrast in polished white stone (11). Rich colours such as these look fantastic in shimmering light-catching silks – here a stripe with a cream ground (8) – or sumptuous velvets (3 and 13). Chic linens or cottons in shades of navy and ubiquitous denim (9 and 12) make a great base for a room. Other textural weaves, such as the wonderful de le Cuona linen-wool-cotton mix in a self-pattern (1) and a basketweave (2), are a good way of using the same colour in a different

texture – and the tweedy blackcurrant knitted fabric (4) can be used as upholstery or for cushion covers to introduce other tones and self-patterns. The subtle narrow stripe (6) is smart and understated, while bolder patterns, such as an ethnic-style print (10) and pretty indigo embroidered Chelsea Textiles fabric (14), go together beautifully and make more of a statement. A nice alternative is one of my absolute favourite fabrics, a sort of tea-stained design that looks close to an antique fabric (7). The marvellous woven leather (15) would be a pleasing modern addition to this scheme.

The subtle tone-on-tone effect is achieved here by using different but equally sumptuous textures. Combinations of rich fabrics such as silks, satins and velvets all work exceptionally well in glamorous deep colours.

Sunflower	Turquoise	Fuchsia
Coral	Silver and Gold	Creamy White

SKY BLUE & GOLD

Jamie Drake's stunning pale sky-blue pieces, which are verging on turquoise, are beautifully set off by the pale walls and dark floor in this room. The addition of mirror and wonderfully aged gilt are perfect accents for the soft blue velvet and pearlescent glass.

VIOLET & TOFFEE

Instead of a coffee table, Stephen Falcke has placed several low wooden stools beside the exceptionally long deep sofa covered in Alcantara (faux suede). The toffee-coloured cushions, in kuba cloth, and the rich wood are a good foil for the stunning violet statement sofa.

DUCK EGG & IMPERIAL YELLOW

In Colette's Lounge at the Grove Hotel, Martin Hulbert's magnificent four-part sofa in deep duck-egg blue fabric by Bruno Triplette is a conversation piece *par excellence*. The silk cushions tone with the sofa and add texture. The sculptural porter chairs, also by Hulbert, were inspired by antique French sedan chairs and have great imperial-yellow cushions – an interesting piece of furniture always makes a great statement.

Accenting blues

BLUE IS SUCH A TRADITIONAL colour and is classically combined or accented with white. But it no longer means just the traditional blue of antique china – it is far more versatile and exciting.

One of the most important accents illustrated here is the combination of imperial yellow with powder blue – an inspired choice. What is far more obvious

but no less beautiful is any of the shades of blue with pink – rose, peony or fuchsia. Silver and gold are, of course, as neutral as can be, and go with blue as they do with every other colour, adding sparkle.

A new entry into the accent stakes is turquoise, an adventurous choice that needs to be used with care. Coral is another new colour to combine with blue, but this can be used with abandon, as it is soft and unthreatening and adds a happy glow to any blue room.

PINKS

PINKS • Cherry Blossom Strawberry Mousse Rose Sweet Pea Raspberry Fool Watermelon Fuchsia Cranberry Strawberry Summer Pudding Cherry Sangria Poppy Rhubarb Claret Plum Mulberry Grape Juice Beetroot Blackberry Aubergine Ruby Merlot Begonia Cassis Salmon Peony Magenta Baby Pink Burgundy Rose Water Red Currant Candy Pink Cyclamen Radish Candyfloss Blush Scarlet Hot Pink Lipstick Beaujolais Crimson

Rich and voluptuous, the new pinks include the wonderful shades of summer flowers and berries – blowsy peonies, overblown roses and juicy strawberries. Many a designer has proved that these shades – from the palest rose or cherry blossom, through vibrant fuchsia and luscious cranberry, to deep aubergine and plum – can be used in many different ways to create stylish and sophisticated rooms.

These Schiaparelli- or fuchsia-pink chairs in the sitting room at the Soho Hotel, London, define the style and ambience of the entire room. Kit Kemp had the upholstery fabric specially made, based on a handbag she owned, and the wool fabric has flowers embroidered on it just as the bag did. The cushions are the same colour but in a different fabric.

CHERRY BLOSSOM

WATERMELON

Think pink! The traditionally feminine hue works its wiles in Jamie Drake's lovely guest room. Floor-to-ceiling colour softens the angular space, while the box-pleated silk pelmets and curtains frame the view. The same slubbed fabric is used for the bed valance and upholstered headboard. Crisp white sheets with a pink border dress the bed. The colour is continued in the room with the pink flowers, lamp and antiqued chest of drawers.

STRAWBERRY MOUSSE

CHERRY BLOSSOM TO FUCHSIA

FUCHSIA

ROSE

SWEET PEA

RASPBERRY FOOL

Once the exclusive preserve of little girls' rooms, pale candy pinks, in a slightly dirty 'off' tone, can actually be used to create beautiful grown-up rooms that are still feminine but very elegant. The brighter shocking-pink shades of fuchsia, cyclamen and watermelon are also surprisingly versatile and provide excitement and impact in a room. These are colours that zing – and they can be used with almost every other colour and shade of pink.

The colours of a garden in summer

WHEN ONE THINKS OF PINK in decorating terms, the traditional image of a girl's bedroom in Barbie pink or the soft tones of a cabbage rose is the look that usually springs to mind. Now, however, in the twenty-first century, 'pink' can mean many more tones, sophisticated as well as exciting.

The cherry blossom-to-fuchsia colour spectrum includes all those shades of pink that for generations have existed in softly patterned chintzes, stripes and checks. They are universal, ever popular and easy to

use in bedrooms and living rooms alike. The big change here is that fabrics in these colours have become more exciting and varied than the traditional cotton and linen – and even include tweed. What is also different is that by using these shades without a great deal of pattern, one can gain a truly soft and gentle perfectly neutral effect in a room that would be pleasing to anyone.

When choosing a shade of pink, select a colour that is suitable for the room in question. Pale, gentle shades of sweet pea and cherry blossom are calming and pretty in a bedroom and can be paired beautifully with deeper tones; while darker shades of rose or watermelon can be used to stunning effect in dining rooms or living areas, as these colours are stimulating and conducive to conversation. The brighter shades of fuchsia and cyclamen can look amazing in bathrooms.

My feeling is that if you are going to use pink, use it with bravura and style rather than with elderly caution. And take advantage of all the wonderful garden flowers to use as accents: add a basket of azaleas and calla lilies, for example, and you have the ultimate pink room.

LEFT The curtain – a de le Cuona fabric – is an almost edible pink tweed, while the chair is upholstered in a cream tweed with a tiny pink fleck running through it. The pink paisley throw with its cream suede fringe ties the two fabrics together. The two tweeds, suede fringe and soft eel-leather cushion add a wonderfully complex feeling of texture.

OPPOSITE Jamie Drake's loft apartment has a relatively open-plan layout, with the dining room adjacent to a magenta-accented living room (see page 138). While the violet-pink of the back wall connects the two spaces, other colours come into play. The wooden floor and curtains are in warm pale gold tones, while iridescent dark slate grey-green chairs surround the patinated steel-finished dining table and a Murano glass chandelier with emerald-green drops hangs above. The antique mirror-fronted sideboard at the back of the room reflects the sculpted table base.

In this great Pink
Salon at the G Hotel
in Galway, Ireland,
designed by Philip
Treacy, the walls
and ceiling are a
wonderful shade
of cyclamen pink,
against which the
metallic sculptures
by David Bartlett
are prominently
displayed. The black
and white carpet was
inspired by a hat
Treacy designed for
Naomi Campbell,
manufactured by
Mac Murray. The
French armchairs
have been painted
white and then
upholstered in an
almost toile-like
fabric in hot pink.
Note the twig mirrors
and Lucite stands
for the sculpture –
great touches in a
room where the
colour is so dynamic.

HOW TO USE BOLD COLOURS – THE NEW PERFECT NEUTRALS

■ The secret to success when using big bold colours as the basis of your scheme is to use them
unapologetically and on a grand scale. As can be seen by Philip Treacy's strong style statement in
the Pink Salon of the G Hotel (above and page 139), fashionable shades of shocking pink can be
used to make great impact in home décor. Here Treacy demonstrates how to pull out all the stops
to create something extremely glamorous – to all lovers of the colour, this is the ultimate pink room.

■ By having almost everything in the room shocking pink – walls, ceiling and upholstery – in a
striking combination of solid colour and tone-on-tone pattern, the space is made exciting but never
jarring, providing a bold but neutral backdrop for a varied collection of furniture and accessories –
black and white, mirror, metal, gilt, glass and acrylic are all perfect accents for a colour such as this.

■ The eclectic use of materials and furniture – the bold rug, the unusual mirrors and sculptures, the
unexpected upholstery – are what give the room drama and glamour and prevent it from looking girlie.

CHERRY BLOSSOM TO FUCHSIA SWATCH GUIDE

A soft rose-coloured limestone (7) is a stunning flooring choice for a pink scheme and prevents the overall effect from looking too girlie. Equally effective is a comfortable deep-pile wool carpet in a warm beige tone (5), while a carpet in a rich pink (2) gives a stronger, more vibrant feel. The gutsy de le Cuona cherry-pink tweed (10) is a wonderful rich fabric that could be used almost anywhere, either alone or in combination with the other de le Cuona

creamy beige tweed with the pink flecks (6) or with the deeper raspberry pink weave (8). These pink textural tweeds create a sophisticated interior. The plain linen (4) and striped fabric (1) would also work well in combination with each other for a classic look, while the traditional pink linen toile (3) gives a more elegant grown-up mood. For a lighter, more feminine touch, try the fine pale pink and white striped voile (9) or the cream silk with embroidered pink roses (11).

A perfect way to use pink is in a stripe. This wonderful fringed tier is a lovely detail.

Designer Stephen Falcke has used a harmonious combination of various tones of red throughout this 1940s Johannesburg house. Eclectic possessions, including African influences plus touches of Tuscany and Provence (favourite holiday destinations of the clients) are united by the colour to create an amazing yet beautifully neutral home. The same red canvas fabric unites the spaces, with occasional stripes, checks and ethnic fabrics.

RHUBARB

POPPY

CHERRY

SUMMER PUDDING

CRANBERRY

CRANBERRY TO RHUBARB

SANGRIA

While many shades of red are often used as accents, working well with rich earth tones as well as with all the greys, decorating an entire room in luscious shades of red may seem like a brave and difficult choice. But, in fact, these colours – cranberry, strawberry and poppy – are perfect neutrals that can be used tone on tone to wonderful effect. Using red successfully is all about a state of mind and a clever mix of tone and texture.

STRAWBERRY

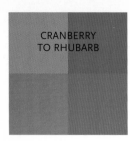

Tone-on-tone reds create a vibrant home

THE ALL-OVER USE OF RED needs careful thought and planning to ensure that the result is liveable and not too strident. I fell in love with this welcoming house in Johannesburg and wanted to understand how its amazing redness had been accomplished to such good effect. I realized that the designer, Stephen Falcke, had achieved a neutral effect by using various tones of red throughout the house with not a single jarring note.

Falcke had worked for the clients before, creating a wonderful French Provençal home for them in a Johannesburg suburb – a large, spacious house with high-ceilinged rooms. This new home, however, was a much smaller 1940s house with an annexe across a courtyard. As such, it presented different challenges and required a totally different look and feel. With Falcke's imagination and flair, the size of the house and the annexe became an asset rather than a liability.

The furniture and accessories are an eclectic mix, but these are beautifully held together by the unified red colour scheme and the clever use of warm, mellow natural materials. Flooring throughout the house is either pale wood or narrow bricks laid in a chevron pattern, then polished and waxed.

ABOVE The entrance to this inviting red house is furnished with a red day bed on which Stephen Falcke has placed a collection of cushions in different red fabrics.

LEFT As in the rest of the house, the curtains are simple red canvas. The bed is made all in white linen – the clients' preference – with a red paisley throw folded across the end of the bed instead of a bedspread. The crystal chandelier is an unexpected change of pace and texture here, and it is touches like this that give the room its character. The original wood floor, stripped and polished, adds warmth.

OPPOSITE The antler chandelier came from the owners' previous home, which had a much higher ceiling. Falcke found a garden table that he stripped, waxed and polished and placed directly under the chandelier, forming a strong focal point for the room. The table houses a collection of African wooden animals. A French day bed sits comfortably close to a chair covered in a Nigerian beaded fabric. There is also an oriental screen, a West African mask and a Zimbabwean woven side table – every piece works with the others in this rich, warm and convivial room.

Outside living is a feature of life in Johannesburg, as there are few months when one cannot sit, eat or gather outside all day and most evenings. These outside living spaces are often spacious and include sitting areas as well as eating and cooking spaces. Note the chevron brick floor – I found these floors to be innovative, inexpensive and quite stunning; and they become warm and inviting with rugs thrown down. Here, the bricks have been glazed to a rich, mellow 'brique' colour – a perfect foil for all the red furniture, which has hints of all the earth colours within its spectrum. The red canvas drapes can be closed on cool evenings. The chair is upholstered in a large red and white gingham check, and the French day bed is in red canvas. Falcke has also introduced several African woven stools and tables.

In order to make this small house flow in a relaxed way from one area to another Falcke used the same red canvas fabric throughout the house – for curtains and for upholstery. To lighten the effect, touches of red and white pattern are brought into play – stripes and checks of various sizes and occasional ethnic fabrics.

As can be seen by the use of red in this house, these strong statement shades are great colours to use for key pieces of furniture in a room. Suddenly red is the colour of choice for upholstered pieces – something that would have been unheard of a few years ago. There should be nothing apologetic about the use of red on furniture: scale is more important than ever, and large and sleek makes the necessary impact.

I recently saw a library in which the wall had been panelled in squares of red leather. This formed the perfect background for everything else in the room, giving it a strong masculine look – but with great style.

USING RED TOP TIPS

■ Stephen Falcke says, 'You need a lot of guts to use red, or no guts at all. Red has a hue and a glow that very few colours have. Food looks at its best in a red dining room.'

■ Use a combination of tones and textures, and introduce patterns in the same palette.

■ Use red with only one or two other shades – say, black, grey and ivory for an elegant, urban look or stone, taupe and coffee for a warmer, softer country feel.

■ Use red accessories – a feathered headdress, glass or ceramics – for vibrant bursts of colour.

CRANBERRY TO RHUBARB SWATCH GUIDE

When it comes to using this vibrant, uplifting colour palette, I suggest taking Stephen Falcke's advice and going in boots and all to create a red, red, red scheme. To that end, I've picked a wonderful selection of fabrics in rich tones of red and in a variety of textures and designs. The star of the scheme has to be the blatantly luxe silk unusually decorated with a latticework of natural string (11) – rather fun. I also love the

unusual irregular pink and red stripe (2), which creates a softer feel, and the wonderful woven deep red leather (12) and crimson faux pony skin (1) for their great, unexpected texture. The herringbone wool weave (4) and rough linens (13 and 15), all in different shades of red, would work especially well with the rough textures of the natural herringbone-patterned sisal flooring (3 and 8), perhaps with a red basketweave

edging in a similar texture (6). Other good flooring options are pale creamy limestone (9) or warm-toned mid-brown oak floorboards (5). The marvellous red paisley on oatmeal (10), chic embroidered motif (14), antique tapestry-style design (16) and conventional 100 per cent wool tartan (7) are all different pattern choices that could be used to create very diverse and distinct looks within a red scheme.

CLARET TO AUBERGINE

CLARET

AUBERGINE

BEETROOT

Another example of a careful selection of different fabrics all in the same shade. An aubergine toile sets the scene – toiles are such good mood-setters, especially in offbeat colours such as this or grey. A stripe adds strength and these chairs look solid, serious and comfortable. The curtains and rug are the same stone shade as the background fabric and are interesting and chic – but perfectly neutral, too.

MULBERRY

PLUM

BLACKBERRY

GRAPE JUICE

These deep berry shades are the richer, more autumnal colours of the pink spectrum that are seen a great deal now. Chic and modern, they blend well and provide a perfectly neutral backdrop with exciting undertones. These colours are a wonderful new look for bedrooms – especially those that are used in a multipurpose way, as so many bedrooms are today. They are also ideal for dining rooms, comfortable family rooms and cosy spaces to curl up in.

Jewel-like colours for a luxurious cocoon

ABOVE Louise Bradley has used different textures in shades of aubergine – on the chair, cushion, platter and glasses. These work well together, giving a mellow hue to the room.

OPPOSITE This mezzanine bedroom/bathroom/dressing area was created by Gérard Faivre for his pied-à-terre in Paris, using rich colour as a contrast to the grey rooms downstairs. The walls are a pale aubergine against which the bed back glows with a deep berry colour; the addition of the red bed cover works superbly well. The floor has been bleached and waxed. The gold Philippe Starck lamp is a glamorous touch.

THERE IS NO DOUBT THAT these colours are hot, hot, hot. They were seen first in high fashion and before long these jewel-like shades emerged on the home scene, too. The colours are as rich as their names suggest: blackberry, cassis, burgundy – all edible again. They suggest velvety, luxurious comfort and tend to make rooms to linger in – as long as they are used with immense care and creativity. Visualize a mixture of berries all piled up together in a glass bowl and you will get the summer look of this colouring; think velvet and silks and deep tones and the mood is warmer, womb-like and cosy. I strongly advise seeking help from a colour specialist, however, as these darker colours can all too easily look heavy and ponderous if overused or used without clever shading.

I can't deny that wonderful effects can be produced with these colours. I have, for example, seen a deep aubergine-purple fabric used as a wall covering for an evening-only dining room and it was glamorous, very grown-up and divine accented with cream lacquer furniture, silver and crystal. Personally, though, I prefer to use these colours as accents rather than as a base for the total scheme of a room, as I find they are colours that can pull a scheme together in an amazing way – they seem to ground it and give it cohesion.

If you wish to go for the full-on effect – and it can certainly look stunning, as these pages testify – bear in mind that somehow in this palette it is very easy to miss the exact, correct and wonderful tone and go for the 'wrong' shades and textures. This can easily make a room look suffocatingly Victorian, so use with caution and if possible get specialist advice. As always, look at large colour swatches in different lights and in different places in the room – sometimes it can be a very subtle variation that makes all the difference.

In terms of fabric choice and textures, a washed velvet from Andrew Martin, rather than a traditional one, has more light and radiance. A cut velvet also

Another view of the aubergine toile in the Soho Hotel in London (see page 132). As well as being used on the walls, the same fabric has been used for a quilt, teamed with crisp white bed linen and a simple Gustavian-like chest used as a bedside table. The main tones from the toile are picked up by the dark headboard and the pale curtains and carpet. Used in this way, the toile gives a soft feminine look with a sense of womb-like comfort: teamed with the stripes, the look was strong and masculine.

works well in these tones. Try a stonewashed linen from de le Cuona, or perhaps even a suede or faux suede. Be adventurous. Toile de Jouy seems to exist in every colour these days – both old designs and new. Many are available in shades of pink – from the palest rose to the deepest plum. Several designers cleverly use toile wallpapers or fabrics on walls and ceilings, which gives an extremely elegant neutral effect. One can either carry on with the same colour spectrum to create a harmonious toile box – with, say, striped and checked fabrics in the same colours and a cream and raspberry carpet – or add some chic contrast. I think the former approach is more effective in this colourway.

Try amethyst glass as an accent – a favourite Nina Campbell look. I like to use rusty metal chandeliers with these colours and, as always, silver finishes and crystal are perfect accessories. Gentle grey or elephant-grey suede envelops the space in yet more quiet luxury.

A WELL-BALANCED BEDROOM STYLE TIPS

■ Choose a colour scheme that is relaxing rather than stimulating. Rich jewel-like colours radiate comfort and intimacy in bedrooms.

■ Bedside lamps with large lampshades make reading in bed impossible and, in my view, they should be banned. Simple stainless-steel or small brass standard lamps that can be swung over and focused on a newspaper or book are elegant and totally practical.

■ Instead of traditional bedspreads that have to be carefully put on each morning and lifted off at night, add colour and texture with layers of linen, wool, cashmere or alpaca; if you want to add pattern, a light toile quilt is ideal.

■ A comfortable upholstered stool at the end of the bed is useful when getting dressed, or for placing books and magazines on.

CLARET TO AUBERGINE SWATCH GUIDE

This is an unusual colour scheme that can look very effective with the right mix of fabrics and colours. A subtle flooring choice would be either limed oak (7) or stone slabs the colour of wet sand (14), while a marvellous veined marble (3) would make a grand statement. In terms of fabric choices, I have gone for a rich mix of weights, from silk velvet (9) and the softest cashmere (15), to linen fabric (6) and ruffled silk taffeta (8), to gauzy sequinned silk (12) and an unusual punctured silky fabric (11), both of which add a certain originality to the scheme. In addition, the ubiquitous leopard has popped up again (13), along with ostrich skin (10) which looks great in the deepest shade of aubergine. As a general rule, I'm not a big lover of pattern, but this silk floral design (2) adds very interesting colours to this mix. I also like the subtle aubergine paisley on a grey linen ground (5), which is almost like a toile. The two different-width stripes (1 and 4) would look fabulous used together.

Accenting pinks

TRADITIONALLY, THE bright shades of pink – the shocking pinks and fuchsias – have tended to be used as accent colours rather than as base colours to be accented. Philip Treacy's Pink Salon at the G Hotel (see opposite and page 124) proves an exception to this rule. In the same way that grey, white and silver look good accented with bright pinks, the reverse is true. The softer peony and rose pinks can be accented with whites and creams for a classic look, but it can be more exciting to use a lime green or even a bright turquoise. If, however, you're looking for complete serenity, once again the best thing is to layer the tones and textures of similar pinks from the palest to the deepest. The exception to this rule is aubergine, which is equally stunning when used on its own and with almost any other colour.

MAGENTA & CHOCOLATE

In this Manhattan living room Jamie Drake has upholstered the sofa in a warm chocolate-brown fabric. The chairs facing it as well as the cushions on the sofa are in magenta. Silver accents are everywhere, adding a cool dimension to this hot, hot room.

CYCLAMEN & IMPERIAL YELLOW

Although it seems as though this room in the G Hotel, designed by Philip Treacy, has a shiny, textured pink wall, it is in fact a metallic wall by David Bartlett, which reflects the pink wall it faces. The Lucite table allows the pink from the skirting board behind to shine through, making this whole area completely pink, apart from the great imperial-yellow modern chair. The flowers, as is so often the case, add the perfect touch – a chunky glass vase of pink roses in a homage to pink.

AUBERGINE & WHITE

The dark, rich aubergine is made soft and feminine by pairing it with crisp white bed linen. I love the addition of the quilted sham pillows – this is a great way to make a bed.

Dark and Light Grey

Acid Green

Turquoise

Maize

Fuchsia

Nutmeg

SUNNY TONES

SUNNY TONES • Sand Hay Peach Sorbet Maize Saffron Sunflower Ochre Topaz Tuscan Wall Paprika Tomato Salsa Burnt Sienna Chilli Pepper Terracotta Bronze Melon Pomegranate Marmalade Sunshine Straw Sun-dried Tomato Squash Pink Champagne Coral Amber Tangerine Barley Glowing Umber Buttercup Candlelight Golden Syrup Primrose Seville Orange Brick Red Conch Shell Parmesan Mango Pumpkin Pie Wheat Field Grapefruit Corn

These are the glorious colours that make a room glow with warmth and light and can bring a sense of permanent sunshine into a home. They can add a smile to your morning and a sense of warmth and comfort to your evening. These colours evoke sun-baked earth in hot climates – the desert sand of Africa, the faded façades of Tuscan towns and the scorching tiles of a Mediterranean terrace.

This sunny guest bedroom designed by Jamie Drake is bright and cheerful, as well as warm and welcoming. The walls are pale tangerine, while the sofa is a deeper burnt-orange velvet. The chair and stool have been given a new lease of life with a smart striped fabric in all shades of the sunny spectrum. A stripe can so often bring colours to earth and add immense flair.

SAFFRON

OCHRE

This is the perfect example of a sunny French tone-on-tone room, where only the textures change. While the basic colour remains the same throughout, the natural-fibre flooring is set against the stone, the silk damask against the distressed wood of the chairs and the chalky walls against the glossy golden fruit-wood furniture. Only the beams are a different colour – dark brown – but blend well with all these sunny tones.

MAIZE

SAND

SAND TO OCHRE

SUNFLOWER

PEACH SORBET

HAY

The pale yellow-based tones of the sunny spectrum are sheer sunshine in a paint tin, bringing instant warmth and light to any room. The soft, gentle shades of sand, maize, hay and straw are really easy to work with and are particularly effective as a backdrop to a room, with either contrasting colour or deeper toning shades. They can be used on large expanses, such as walls, floor or curtains, to create subtle glowing planes.

Bathe your home in permanent sunshine

THESE PALE SUNNY TONES are some of the easiest neutral shades to use, as not only do they complement the darker colours of the spectrum – the topaz to terracotta palette – they also tend to go with most of the other groups of perfect neutrals. And what permeates every room based on this palette is, without doubt, the sensation of sun, warmth and happiness.

Conventionally, these sunny maize tones work very well with off-whites and creams, as well as with the earth and spice spectrum – cinnamon and ginger or, for a more wintry feel, shades of coffee and chocolate. For those who wish to be more adventurous, however, maize and heather can make a remarkable combination

that is exciting as well as pleasingly neutral. The yellow cats – leopard, cheetah and tiger – are all wonderful as accents, while light woods, such as fruit wood, and painted white furniture work particularly well in this colour spectrum.

Used extensively for walls, floors or soft furnishings, these gentle yellow colours provide a calm, uplifting backdrop for bedrooms, living rooms, kitchens and bathrooms. The colours work tonally with interesting natural floors, which are a practical choice for kitchens and bathrooms. Together with stone sinks and bathtubs, these floors look stunning teamed with ochre paint – with real pigment for a moody effect.

Using these neutral sunny colours as a base for a room gives one the opportunity to add colour and excitement with fabrics in patterns such as paisleys, toiles, stripes, checks or florals in slightly deeper shades, or even in a completely different colour. These can be used effectively and in combinations for upholstery, curtains or cushions. Also ideal for this colour scheme is a beautiful wallpaper collection by Carleton V, which is almost like a reverse toile de Jouy and comes with a matching fabric. Used for walls and drapes, the ethereal Jasper Peony in Georgian yellow would create the perfect mellow background for a room decorated in this colour scheme. The concept of reversing a toile – with the stronger colour being the background and the design depicted in a paler shade – works really well for a neutral effect.

OPPOSITE The wonderful pale gold silky drapes generously enclosing this reproduction French trundle bed are a Fortuny fabric in a similar shade to the wall behind. The cushions are made from old patterned fabrics in warm ochre and faded peach colours. Even the parrot tulips are the same sunny tones used throughout the room.

CENTRE Designer Frank Faulkner has chosen a soft maize colour for the walls, an unusual but effective neutral on which to base a living room. The white paintwork and off-white upholstery give a fresh, summery feel.

ABOVE This simple bedroom in a hunting lodge in Périgord, France, is decorated in gentle tones of yellow that are typical of the area. The colour blends beautifully with the warm tones of the wood on the ceiling, floor and bed frame, and lightens the room, giving it a warm golden glow.

LEFT This very chic but comfortable room designed by Nancy Braithwaite is warmed with shades of pale gold smartly accented with black. This works very well with the rich dark wooden furniture. The windows are dressed with softly pleated curtains in alternating gold and black, while the pale gold chairs are finished with black trim.

BELOW This bedroom, bathed in saturated golden yellow tones, is as warm as sunshine itself. The curtains are a slightly darker shade than the upholstery and walls, adding depth to the room. The leopard- and tiger-print rug adds a touch of contemporary chic.

USING YELLOW TOP TIPS

■ Sumien Brink, Editor of *Visi* magazine in Cape Town, says that sunny yellow is one of the most uplifting colours there is. It is joyful, friendly, open and outgoing, and brings a feeling of hope and an air of radiance.

■ Yellow stimulates the brain and makes people open-minded, decisive and alert. It helps concentration and is therefore a good colour to use in rooms where you work or think, so it's ideal for a home office or study.

■ It is an excellent colour to highlight a focal point and draw the eye and can be combined successfully with harmonizing or contrasting tones.

■ Yellow is an ideal colour for interiors and exteriors alike, and can make any area warm and inviting. Too much bright yellow can make you nervous or irritated, so stick to buttery yellows or ochres.

SAND TO OCHRE SWATCH GUIDE

Here is a harmonious selection of fabrics and materials for a sunny yellow scheme, with a choice of mellow cherry-stained oak flooring (2), warm sandy stone (12), golden corn-coloured carpet (1) and the great striped carpeting (3) that I love to use on stairs and down hallways. A rug in a rough texture such as sisal, with a sand-coloured basketweave edging (13), would

also work very well in a pale sunny scheme. Leopard (7), ostrich (8) and a leather or suede fabric in a rich amber colour that would tie in beautifully with the cherry-wood floor (4) all provide marvellous texture. The wonderful tweedy dark cream fabric (14), together with the textural stripe with tan and black running through it (6) would be great choices for upholstery – as

would the watered-silk chenille (9), which also adds a touch of luxury and has a lovely sheen when the light falls on it. The wide silk stripe (10) would make sumptuous curtains, while the maize fabric with a flower design embroidered in string (5) and the gentle leaf-print cotton-linen mix (11) could be used to introduce more pattern in the form of cushions or drapes.

CHILLI PEPPER

This room is colourful yet neutral and original. For the walls Jamie Drake has used a stunning parchment paper by Elizabeth Dow, which comes in seven sunny shades from cantaloupe to fire-engine red. The blinds are in the darker shades of the wallpaper and the cushion on the maize chair is a deeper shade of reddish terracotta. Dark browns can be found in the rug and on the sofa, picture frames and unusual table.

PAPRIKA

TOPAZ

BURNT SIENNA

TUSCAN WALL

TOPAZ TO TERRACOTTA

TOMATO SALSA

The darker tones in this spectrum – burnt sienna, brick red and terracotta – are ultimate neutrals and almost foolproof to use: think of the rich colours of Tuscan houses and landscapes. The paler and brighter shades, however, require caution – a little paint goes a long way. There are some great fabrics in this colour spectrum – for example, Olivier Desforges's range of stripes, checks and self-patterns – which make it easy to 'do' a room in these colours.

TERRACOTTA

Deep sunny tones for informal elegance

I HAVE ALWAYS LOVED what I think of as the colours of Italian limewashed walls. The tones are rich yet not heavy; neutral but not dull; and exciting without being psychedelic. The darker shades have the advantage of being very easy to use and difficult to make errors with, as long as one chooses good-quality paints in true 'off' colours. The brighter tones of pomegranate, chilli pepper, tangerine and cantaloupe require a little

more skill. In my opinion, these shades are best used in sunny parts of the world, where the sun has the effect of bleaching out colour to a certain extent. In cooler climates, unless used with delicacy and expertise, these vibrant colours can look heavy and overpowering. Look to Jamie Drake for inspiration, as he uses this colour scheme all over a room for a perfectly neutral effect but with enormous pizzazz (see page 148).

RIGHT In this chic dining room, the cream walls, stone fireplace, wooden table and tall metal candlesticks are offset by the richest of brick-red shades used for the chairs, table runner and napkins, tied with paisley fabric. This elegant yet informal style of table dressing is favoured by Bernie de le Cuona. For this autumnal setting she has run a long folded throw down the length of the table and laid the plates straight on the wood. Simple cutlery and large gilt-rimmed glasses complete the effect. A wooden bowl filled with red apples adds to the rustic mood.

LEFT AND BELOW The paprika walls in this suite at the Soho Hotel, designed by Kit Kemp, are a soft washed-out shade with a fine pigment, and are paired with white skirting boards and cornices – a great look. This strong bright colour has been teamed with a new and unusual striped upholstery fabric – a pale sand colour with dark slate-grey and cream stripes. The combination of colours on the cushions serves to pull the scheme together. The chic contemporary look is reinforced by the clean-lined pale wooden furniture, which works far better than dark mahogany would. The animal-hide rug in the seating area complements the colour scheme and adds a real up-to-the-minute touch, while the dark frames, lamps and table echo the slate stripe and help to anchor the room.

The colours that fall into the deeper sunny-tones spectrum – topaz to terracotta – are wonderfully new and exciting shades to be considered perfect neutrals. The strong intense colours such as paprika and brick are uplifting but stimulating rather than soothing, so I find they are best suited to convivial areas such as living rooms and dining rooms, while the paler shades of Tuscan wall and pink champagne create a warm, calm feel that is perfect for sultry bedrooms. The russet tones of burnt sienna and terracotta evoke winter warmth, especially when used in rich or textured fabrics. These shades are ideal for rustic interiors, as they combine well

RIGHT The walls in this nineteenth-century dining room by Frank Faulkner are a rich coral, sponged to create texture and shade. This strong colour is offset by the crisp white-painted ceiling and Queen Anne-style chairs. The pale floor has been sponged and divided into a grid in an imitation of limestone.

OPPOSITE Designers Coorengel and Calvagrac have used a colour with a real eighteenth-century Neapolitan feel. The wall colour is Clair de Lune by Ressource, the silk curtains are by Jim Thompson and the antique bed is upholstered in pure silk with a Greek-key binding. A cinnamon-brown faux-fur throw adds glamour. Objects and paintings seem to be randomly grouped but have actually been chosen with real care. I love the black and white veined marble urn in the corner; don't forget black – it is a great accent colour.

with dark stone and wood. The lighter tones are effective in clean-lined contemporary settings, as they create a fresh, crisp, summery look that is still comfortable and welcoming. The scope is vast and, of course, the choice of fabrics and accents can change the look completely.

Once considered purely Tuscan or at least Italian in spirit, terracotta is now one of the most popular neutral shades to use worldwide. It has everything: warmth, sunshine and a sense of Italian chic that travels well. It is a subtle colour that blends or highlights and can be used as a background colour to many different accent shades. Find a tone you truly love in an antique rug or fragment of tile: the older the item is, the more the

colour will have faded and mellowed, and this should be the look you aim for in your scheme – a weathered look is so often the best way to go. Sunny terracotta kitchens, with lots of yellow-coloured wood, are a welcome change from ubiquitous stainless steel.

Burnt sienna is another colour that is equally good as a basic perfect neutral and as an accent. As with burgundy and aubergine, however, when using this shade as a base colour, great care is required to find exactly the right shade. I like it very burnt-looking, teamed with walnut wood, brass studs and lots of black and silver. When used as an accent colour, burnt sienna is almost as universally perfect as acid green

for adding excitement and flavour. The expected creams and coffee colours are its most perfect partners, but the right shade of burnt sienna can also be teamed successfully with many other colours.

In all their variations of tone and shade, rich sunny colours work extremely well with natural materials such as stone, slate, brick and wood – not to mention animal hides, making it a truly of-the-moment palette. An exciting aspect of twenty-first-century design is the emergence of wonderful new natural stone materials that can be used in building and decorating. The choice of colours and textures seems endless – hematoid quartz, for example, is perfect for this colour scheme.

USING DEEP SUNNY TONES TOP TIPS

■ Sumien Brink suggests using uplifting, friendly shades of burnt orange and terracotta in a kitchen. As well as being associated with creativity, these colours stimulate and aid conversation.
■ Rich shades of red are energizing and promote movement and activity. Use these colours in playrooms, kitchens, entrance halls and dining rooms. They can be dramatic, opulent and seductive. When used sparingly on a feature wall, deep reds can be very sophisticated.

This smart seating area has a distinctly Chinese feel, with the framed calligraphy forming a focal point on the wall and providing the springboard for the bold and decisive use of black, white and tomato red. The room has a strong linear quality, with the hard angles of the dark table and the L-shaped seating reinforced by the black and white striped curtains and cushions, and by the use of horizontal bands of colour on the sofa.

TOPAZ TO TERRACOTTA SWATCH GUIDE

It must be obvious that I'm not overly keen on patterned fabrics but occasionally a stripe (7 and 5) or a tone-on-tone pattern such as a paisley (2 and 13) can be very effective in small doses. Even a bold monochrome (14) can work well if used sparingly and balanced with plains in various textures, such as soft suede (1)

and velvety textures (4 and 9). The wide striped silk, which incorporates wonderful rich shades of pink and purple (5), would make stunning curtains for a large window; a pattern such as this needs space to breathe and to have full impact. The narrower stripe (7) is ideal for upholstery or cushion covers. I love leathers

and animal skins, such as this ostrich (12) which adds pattern and texture to the scheme. For flooring I suggest a stone floor (8) or copper-coloured bamboo (10). Or go for sisal in a russet shade (3), perhaps with a herringbone edging (11), or a terracotta-coloured short-pile wool carpet (6).

Accenting sunny tones

AS IN SO MANY CASES, it is the shades found
in nature that work well both as base colours for a
room and as accents. Whenever I interview designers,
they all talk about how safe it is to use natural shades
for decorating, so it is not surprising to find that slate,
coffee, terracotta, maize and paprika are the preferred
accent colours for this section. Coffee, anthracite and
deep terracotta tend to make a room slightly warmer
and suitable for winter. Whereas using the lighter,
fresher tones, such as white, maize, tangerine and
peach, creates a spring-like feel.

Don't forget displays of flowers or fruit as very
important accents in any room. Both are delightful
used in abundance in sunny rooms – whether large
vases of cut sunflowers, mimosa or parrot tulips, or
huge piles of rosy apples or a simple basket of lemons.

Coffee Beans   **Wicker**   **Terracotta**

**Brushed
Aluminium**   **Slate**   **Ebony**

SAND, SUNFLOWER, TERRACOTTA & SAGE

This scene suggests a perfect sunny day in the South of France. The room is a mellow mix of sunny tones – sand, sunflower and terracotta – with touches of pale sage and warm wood tones. The sandy walls and French country table are accented with the great yellow plates that are typical of the area, the vase of sunflowers, the yellow blinds with terracotta pelmets and the painted chairs. The soft sage napkins echo the pattern on the plates.

BRICK RED & COFFEE BEANS

Brick red is a wonderful wintry accent with all the sunny tones from the palest sand to terracotta. These rich-coloured linen napkins add a zesty look to a simple dark brown wooden dining table.

PARMESAN, SLATE & STRING

The maize walls are the perfect backdrop to the white-painted woodwork and furniture and the mellow wood of the floor. The slate accent is a smart touch, while the collection of black and white prints framed in black add a sense of gravitas to the room.

EARTH AND SPICE • Camel Latte Brown Bread Malted Milk Praline Truffle Mushroom Mole Ginger Muscovado Sugar Cognac French Mustard Mocha Caramel Cinnamon Toffee Saddle Brown Gingerbread Molasses Coffee Beans Chocolate Whisky Honey Butterscotch Rye Bread Cappuccio Burnt Almond Fudge Toast Fawn Taupe Ecru Cep Nutmeg Mud Tan Hazelnut Tortoiseshell Bulrush Cocoa Horse Chestnut Peanut Shell Earthenware

Like the neutrals in the very first chapter, 'Off-whites', the earth and spice colours are possibly the most straightforward to use when decorating. These are the colours of warm wood and natural fibres, so it is almost impossible to make a serious error when decorating with them. The downside is that it's all too easy to make rooms in these tones look bland – how you use them makes all the difference.

This kitchen in a Manhattan loft, designed by Clodagh, is a warm, inviting mélange of all the earth and spice tones. Several different tones and types of wood have been used for the kitchen units and counter, floor, table and bench seating. The various shades blend harmoniously to create a truly mellow area in which one could happily cook, eat and chat.

CAMEL

BROWN BREAD

This loft living area is not light and feminine, but a comfortable, elegant, usable space that capitalizes on the warmth and strength of this earthy palette with a mix of wood and fabric in varying tones. The cappuccino and cream upholstery works well with the gingery-taupe walls. The wooden tables are heavy and linear with toning accessories. Note the curtainless windows with simple gauze linen blinds.

MALTED MILK

PRALINE TRUFFLE

CAMEL
TO MOLE

MOLE

LATTE

MUSHROOM

These colours are conventional neutral shades that can be used to create classic interiors that are warm, cosy and inviting. But it is how they are being used today that makes them chic and different. Once again, layering these shades from palest to darkest and adding the *frisson* through textural changes makes for a hospitable and interesting room; then add unusual accents such as lime green, Chinese red or turquoise for an extra 'wow' factor.

CAMEL
TO MOLE

RIGHT Vicente Wolf
has used creamy
upholstery as his
accent colour in this
dark camel and
mocha room – it is
the salt to his spice.
The large curved
settee is the main
focus of the room
but the cream chair
throws it into strong
relief, as does the
mocha ottoman. A
further layer of colour
is provided by the
brass and wood on
the ottoman.

OPPOSITE In this
bedroom Larry Laslo
has created a perfect
haven – comfortable
and warm in rich
shades of camel and
coffee, from latte
to cappuccino to
macchiato, and
neither strongly
masculine nor
feminine in feel.
The iron bedstead
is an unexpected
yet effective contrast
to all the softness of
the wool, cashmere
and fine Frette
sheets. The shearling
bedspread is a great
choice for winter
warmth and mellow
tones. The rich
cream hangings with
coffee trim are the
perfect accent.

The classic colours of comfort

COMBINING ALL THE PALE camel, coffee and mushroom shades, from the darkest mole to the lightest cappucino froth, and then adding brown sugar and a touch of cream creates a wonderful palette that is elegant and modern yet completely neutral. With these harmonious tones as your base, it's hard to go wrong. You can use any number of different shades to make the scheme varied and interesting – say, a string-coloured upholstered settee; an ottoman in oatmeal tweed; cinnamon walls; ginger or sand silk blinds over sheer linen ones; different stripes and plains for cushions; and a great natural wooden floor, perhaps with a string-coloured cotton or wool rug. Add large

paintings or black and white photographs to introduce some drama and always choose your accessories with care, as these will add richness and style to the room.

Natural surfaces work especially well with this colour palette, and I don't think there has ever been such a great collection of woods, stones, granites and glass available for use as floors, wall coverings and other surfaces around the home. Used cleverly, these materials can add enormous interest to an interior and are the ideal solution with earth shades. Don't forget Corian, either – although it's not natural, it looks it and now comes in the most amazing patterns and colours, such as Pompei red, terra, Sahara and cocoa brown.

In this earth-toned bathroom, with its warm glowing planes of the sink unit and splashback and the natural wood storage and bench, the floor is a cool blue-grey stone, which is also a feature of the multicoloured stone tile wall at the back. The contrast between the warm and cool shades is striking and gives the room a very unusual look.

Sleek glass walls – either sheets of reinforced glass, mosaic tile or glass bricks – look chic with many earth colours and make a truly modern statement. Glass can be a very lustrous choice and is great for splashbacks.

Wood is a true designer solution today and can be used everywhere, from open beams to furniture, from turned objects to doors and floors. Available in so many colours and finishes, it's a material that can solve endless design problems and take many guises.

When it comes to using natural materials, think laterally. I have recently seen a narrow terracotta brick, usually used for driveways, employed as interior flooring (see pages 11 and 130). Stone can often be cold, but these chevron-patterned bricks with a coat of glaze are warm and inviting. I have seen leather on walls and reinforced glass as kitchen worktops, while iron chairs – antique, contemporary or garden – look amazing in a sophisticated room, with a cushion for a medieval look.

CAMEL TO MOLE TOP TIPS

■ This palette works equally well in the city and country. Interior designer Jean Larette would use it anywhere from a glass-fronted high-rise apartment to an Arts and Crafts-style bungalow.

■ It lives with Ralph Lauren plaids as easily as with William Morris florals and Andrew Martin tribal-inspired cottons and jutes.

■ This is not a palette for a beach house – its warmth is meant for a colder climate, with sumptuous fabrics, a roaring fire and a perfect cognac. It should be layered and lush, and invites you to nestle under a cashmere throw.

CAMEL TO MOLE SWATCH GUIDE

This is a very sober, muted palette, with flooring in either pale limestone (9), oatmeal wool carpeting (13) or rustic natural-fibre flooring in dark brown (7) or beige (3). The flooring doesn't want to deviate too much from the predominant colours and textures used in the room, as this is what makes an interior decorated in these colours so calming and harmonious. A combination of fine silk fabrics such as a plain mushroom (2) and a wide stripe in cream and mushroom (11) can be used alone or with a heavier mole suede (1) and a coarse linen weave (14) to add textural as well

as tonal variety. The chestnut velvet square fabric (8) has a wonderful geometric quality as well as a great texture. The giraffe print (4) also adds an interesting geometric punch to the scheme, as does the emu leather in a lovely rich dark brown (12). When decorating with a colour palette such as this, you need to be wary of the room becoming too monochrome. The softest touch of 100 per cent cashmere in duck-egg blue (6) or deep saddle-brown (10) adds nice colour. The blue cashmere, used in combination with the textured stripe (5), would undoubtedly give the scheme a welcome lift.

Three different textures – wood, stone and fabric – in very similar but subtly different camel shades work together to create a harmonious scheme.

The walls of Eldo Netto's formal but comfortable bedroom are covered in a wonderful burnt-cinnamon velvet, which brings a rich tone and texture to the room. The golden colours of the wooden floor and furniture blend perfectly with this wall colour. The blue of the picture mount is brought into play by a large floral linen chintz that is used on the other side of the bedroom (not shown).

MOCHA

MUSCOVADO SUGAR

COGNAC

CARAMEL

GINGER TO CINNAMON

CINNAMON

GINGER

The more lively shades of the earth and spice spectrum are the exotic colours of Morocco and Italy. These vibrant colours look best in sunny climates or in light-filled rooms, which prevent them from seeming too heavy, but they can also be used successfully in sophisticated urban settings. Truly versatile, they work well in luxury fabrics and in unusual combinations, but they are more difficult to work with than the other palettes in this spectrum.

FRENCH MUSTARD

RIGHT The walls of this bedroom are lined with squares of ginger leather for a soft, tactile effect. Alberto Pinto has chosen a modern carpet that blends pefectly with the colour on the walls, the rust-coloured bed and the mocha throw. The striking mirror is by Hervé van der Straeten.

OPPOSITE This room by Vicente Wolf exhibits not only a superb use of colour but also an ability to add elements of interest and age to give any room an understated 'wow' factor. The rich spicy tones of the armchair upholstery juxtapose with the much lighter skirt. These comfortable armchairs have been teamed with Chinese period chairs with imperial-yellow seats – a great accent for this mellow spice-coloured room. The carpet and curtains are a lighter shade of spice and the drapes are simple silk taffeta with sheer blinds beneath.

Spicy tones create a vibrant mood

I LOVE THESE RICH EARTH colours as they are used on the outsides of buildings in such places as Arizona, New Mexico and Africa. They suit modern buildings as well as traditional curved adobe houses and make even austere shapes look welcoming. In Johannesburg I have seen these colours and finishes taken inside the home and given a rough, almost ethnic finish as a backdrop to African art; it looks amazing with wood and iron furniture and ceramics.

The rich and mellow hues of stone used on floors or walls add a restful feel to a room decorated in this colour palette and provide the perfect earthy base for soft furnishings in vibrant spicy colours such as ginger, cumin and cinnamon. The fact that stone is a natural material and solidly earthy seems to add a sense of

integrity. It seems that natural materials are becoming more and more sought after in twenty-first-century living. Recently, in both South Africa and in the southern USA, I found that many contemporary designers were looking at exciting ways of using different types of stone – for instance, brick, limestone, travertine and slate – as floors in domestic interiors.

There are other wonderful materials used in building and decorating that naturally bring all the earth shades into play. I saw plaster being applied in Johannesburg that dried to the colour of warm earth and required no paint finish at all – its inherent dull taupe colour was perfect. Old worn floorboards can have a similar effect, as can stone slab floors or waxed bricks, which work especially well in warm climates or in outdoor

settings. Texture becomes even more significant when colours are muted earth tones and is the element that can change the emphasis of a room.

The other obvious flooring choice is natural waxed wood, as the golden tones are the perfect complement to the colours in this spectrum. I love the way rich leather sofas in warm gingery brown stand firmly on wooden floors in glowing caramel tones, while tables sit alongside in a shade somewhere in between the two. All you need is a cowhide rug on the floor and a great textural throw for a truly modern neutral look.

I have seen a definite move towards interesting colour combinations in bedrooms and many designers are using the earth and spice colours in imaginative and inspiring ways. In an era when bedrooms are often multipurpose – places for reading, studying, watching TV and listening to music as well as for sleeping – earth and spice colours seem to me to be a perfect choice, bridging the gap betwen living and sleeping and creating the ideal mood in which to do both.

Think about using bronze as an accent with these colours – it is subtle and rich and adds real excitement if used in interesting ways. In a kitchen try copper pots and pans – either new Californian or French ones or old battered flea-market or antiques shop finds.

ABOVE Luigi Esposito has adorned this four-poster bed from Thailand with a patchwork quilt and a myriad cushions in all the great spicy autumn colours. These were designed by Katharine Pooley using antique kimonos found on her travels; together with the blind and pagoda lampshades, they help to turn this room into an exotic Eastern refuge. The carpet is soft ginger while the wenge chair, with chocolate cushions, is the accent in this room.

USING SPICY TONES TOP TIPS

■ Antiques dealer and interior designer Diana Sieff suggests emphasizing texture and luxury.
■ For a study in this beautiful warm palette, start with cinnamon polished-plaster walls, a perfect background for a mix of antique and modern pieces in chocolate leather and dark walnut. Add iron wall sconces and cumin linen shades, with smart reclaimed parquet flooring topped with an antique silk Persian rug.
■ In a living space window treatments should be sumptuous with a masculine twist – mole velvet drapes edged in mocha silk with ginger and caramel wide-stripe Roman blinds – with a large sofa in chocolate-brown silk velvet and antique tapestry cushions, with dark red worn leather chairs and an old mirrored coffee table.

ABOVE This cognac-coloured veined-marble bathroom looks warmer than stark white and more masculine. The large silver bowl of natural sponges in both similar and contrasting shades adds a practical and stylish note to this über-chic bathroom.

GINGER TO CINNAMON SWATCH GUIDE

These are rich glowing tones that work well with earthy floors and carpets, such as ginger polished stone (7), a rich rust and natural sisal (13) or a pale camel bamboo (8) for a lighter look. For a little pattern underfoot, there is the spicy stripe that is so good for stairs and hallways (1). Rich colours look great in equally rich textures, so I have selected bold ginger leather (5) and antiqued hide (10) along with silk velvet (3), chinchilla (4) and a light sheer (9). In terms of pattern, there are the safer choices of a silky cinnamon self-pattern (12) or a burnt-orange fabric with geometric embroidery in string (2). But for a bolder look, go for an animal print, such as this ginger and black faux leopard skin (11) and a wonderful Hollyhock design (6), which features touches of duck-egg blue and pinky browns that look great with these colours.

GINGERBREAD

CHOCOLATE

The inviting oversized mattresses are upholstered in chocolate alpaca. The other pieces of furniture are all shades of this same colour but in different tones and fabrics – silk taffeta, velvet, wool, cotton faille, leather and cowhide. The walls are in a textured cotton fabric in a similar shade, creating a cocoon effect. The old Chinese lattice windows on the wall add liveliness, ensuring the monochrome room is varied and exciting.

TOFFEE

SADDLE BROWN

RYE BREAD

TOFFEE TO CHOCOLATE

MOLASSES

COFFEE BEANS

Warm, inviting and cocoon-like, these are the colours to welcome you home on a cold evening. You need only add a touch of these classic wintry shades to change the mood of a room with the seasons. The rich warm tones are adaptable to every texture, every fabric and almost every decorating style. But as before, it is how you use these shades that will determine whether your room is conventionally dull or brilliantly original.

Add warmth with rich chocolate tones

RICH SHADES OF BROWN are in vogue for the home as well as for the wardrobe. Used in a textural open-weave fabric and teamed with black, chic chocolate tones can be Milan-smart. And although these are classic cold-weather colours, they can also be very effective in warm sunny climates. Nothing much can surpass dark chocolate or mocha wool in the warmth stakes: in leather, nubbly wool, faux or real fur and fine wools, this palette is perfect for winter – with

burnt orange as a great accent. But today shades of deep brown can be as summery as you wish, simply depending on how you use them. Dark chocolate linen makes a perfect neutral base colour that works with virtually every other major colour group. My favourite partners are ochre, maize, terracotta and all the many shades of stone and cream.

In my view, leather always looks best in the darkest coffee brown – and this applies to shoes and handbags as well as furniture. More and more I am seeing wonderful upholstered leather furniture in dark mahogany brown. I like this best used with coffee shades or with the sunny terracotta spectrum, but it is so neutral that it can be used in almost any scheme. Leather is also increasingly being used as a luxury wall covering, and for desks and tables as well as for chairs.

Using conventional fabrics in unexpected ways adds an element of surprise to a room. Introducing unusual, even seemingly unsuitable, fabrics into perfect neutral schemes can also be very effective.

TOFFEE TO CHOCOLATE

ABOVE Stripes are my favourite contrast fabric, as they always work and are now available in the most amazing colours. Like this stripe used by Kit Kemp at the Soho Hotel, London, they are no longer predictable but are full of 'off' colours and interesting shades, adding a new dimension to any scheme. In this particular example the addition of teal and aubergine to the earth/spice stripe is pure genius.

LEFT A welcoming outside/inside living space in Johannesburg has been created by Stephen Falcke with gunmetal woven furniture and cushions covered in a neutral caramel shade of sailcloth. The ferns in the glasses, the large glass-topped tables and heavy carved wooden African bowls all add great texture to the space.

Corduroy, in any of the wide range of lush coffee and chocolate tones, is wonderfully textural. In some of the softer and more feminine shades this heavy-duty fabric can add an amazing level of sophistication, as well being practical and hard-wearing.

Perfect for adding instant texture are fabrics that are sold by the metre ready-pleated and tucked. These make excellent cushions and bedspreads and can also be used to upholster small items such as stools.

Silk taffeta always imparts a very special level of luxury to a room. I particularly love the look and feel of silk taffeta curtains – both lined and unlined, they add glamour and quality to any scheme. The fabric should 'puddle' to the floor rather than just skim it.

Linens are essential – but how about introducing some of the wonderful new mattress tickings, by Ralph Lauren for example? These come in shades of the same colour or in contrasting colours for a more zingy look.

As I have mentioned, animal skins, both real and artificial, are *de rigueur*, and there are also countless

ABOVE LEFT This is one of my favourite colour combinations – bright orange, brick red or burnt sienna with a mellow earth palette. Bernie de le Cuona has added cushions in oatmeal linen, chocolate suede and flame orange to a sofa in a deep fig brown. Further colour, pattern and texture are brought into play with tartan wool throws on the seat and arm, and an elegant oatmeal throw across the antique leather trunk.

ABOVE Under an African mirror are a pile of cushions that provide an easy way to make an instant transformation to a room – a seasonal change or a new look – without any serious upheaval. The hound's-tooth cushion is topped with one in a tribal beaded linen fabric, with a great tassel.

OPPOSITE In this earth and spice room in the Soho Hotel, the walls have been painted in a warm pale whisky shade that brings all the other tones used into strong relief. The sofa is covered in a heavy stone linen with a flower outline in the colour of gingerbread – so chic. This new type of tone-on-tone pattern is ideal for a perfect neutral scheme. The sturdy wood furniture is a great accent for this palette.

USING RICH EARTH-SPICE TONES TOP TIPS

■ San Franciscan-based interior designer Jean Larette suggests accenting an earthy palette with a soft sage green to add warmth; painting woodwork in dove white will create drama and frame the coloured walls. Walls can be covered in burlap for texture and depth.

■ Furniture finished in espresso brown and stark black creates a stunning contrast when placed in earth-toned settings.

■ Earthy burgundy and rich caramel work beautifully in layers of plush velvet, luxurious mohair, fine cashmere and silky golden trim.

■ Spicy mustards and burnt cinnamon are at home with objects and artwork from cultures as diverse as the Far East, tribal Africa and the bungalows of Berkeley, California.

chic by-product animal-skin upholstery fabrics and rugs. By this I mean ostrich skin, leather, cowhide and sheepskin that are by-products of the meat for which these animals are bred. I have been told that the infinitely fashionable zebra skins are from culls of these animals, but I find the by-product skins more ethically acceptable.

Natural-looking weaves are also increasingly seen in interiors as a contrast to some of the very complicated fabric compositions of recent years. These can be used to add a quite different dimension to the overall feel of a perfectly neutral room, where texture is so very important in providing definition, contrast and excitement.

Quilted fabrics are another way of achieving this textural interest. Not only are they classic choices for bed coverings, quilted fabrics can be used to make luxurious curtains and sumptuous upholstery, too.

TOFFEE TO CHOCOLATE SWATCH GUIDE

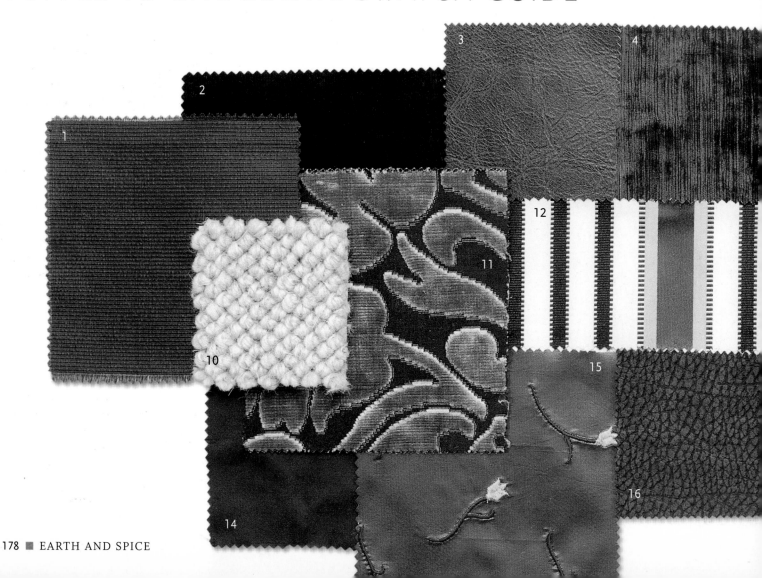

A stately distressed leather Chesterfield sofa by Ralph Lauren gives a clubby look to this London penthouse overlooking the Thames. Luigi Esposito has combined comfort with a real contemporary feel throughout. The teaming of distressed dark toffee-brown leather with handmade 100 per cent cashmere and wool cushions and throws is a great success. I love the use of faux suede on the walls and the taupe velvet on the chair – it's a mix that works.

This palette creates a strong masculine look that is also very warm and rich. Unlike the darker end of the grey spectrum, where I chose predominantly masculine fabrics, here I suggest using soft dark chocolate cashmere (2), rich velvety stripes (4) and patterns (11), textured checks (13) and a ribbed silk (1), which all blend well with the different shades, textures and finishes of the leathers chosen (3, 9 and 16). The leopard print (7) adds a frivolous, fashionable touch of pattern. The lighter-weight fabrics, such as the silky plain chocolate fabric (14), the pretty floral embroidered fabric (15) and the chic black, white and brown stripe (12) give a less wintry feel. Used in combination with the ubiquitous oatmeal linen (8), these fabrics could easily take this colour palette through the summer months without it feeling too oppressive. In terms of flooring, rich polished dark oak (5) looks fantastic, while extra comfort and warmth can be added with a sumptuous creamy carpet or rug (10), while the pale sisal (6) gives a more summery mood.

Piedmontese
Auberbgine

Mixed Peppers

White

Chinese Yellow

Acid Green

Pillow Blue

Accenting earth tones

SOFT TEAL BLUE LOOKS so at home against earth
tones, as illustrated here; it seems to be a magnificent,
if unusual, way of giving them a sophisticated urban
look. Other modern ways of accenting earth and spice
colours are with acid greens and yellows, as they, too,
add a cosmpolitan, urban edge to these traditional
tones. It is perhaps best to use them in small doses, such
as cushions and accessories, rather than in big expanses.

  More conventional ways of accenting these colours
are by using pale and rich terracotta shades – Alberto
Pinto uses pale terracotta and black, for example – or
trying the deep, dark chocolate colours and perhaps
even a very pale lavender or soft aubergine.

TOFFEE, TURQUOISE & CREAM

Seagrass chairs are accented with pure silk velvet cushions, which could be considered a very unexpected combination of textures. The pale turquoise looks lovely with the brown and cream tones used in this room.

COCOA, MUSHROOM & TEAL

The traditional masculine-looking buttoned leather chairs are given an update and a feminine touch with the addition of a mushroom cushion and a teal silk tasselled cushion.

PALE CINNAMON & CREAM

The woven wood panel walls of Alberto Pinto's library are pale cinnamon; the upholstery is cream and the carpet features both shades. The hand-painted leather seats of the eighteenth-century gilt chairs add another dimension.

SAND, CINNAMON & LAVENDER

Barbara Barry designed these stunning chairs that Stephen Falcke has covered in lavender. This is an unusual colour to have chosen for a room where there is so much wood but it works extremely well. The vibrant Paul Smith rug and Falcke's eclectic accessories – oriental screens, African artefacts and a great sculpture – tie all the colours together.

GINGER & SEAGRASS

Luigi Esposito uses seagrass a great deal, as it works as a good contrast to dark wood furniture. Here, this seagrass console displays an ethnic wooden bowl filled with eggs made from fragments of eggshell; its rough texture is juxtaposed with the lush softness of the rich fur throw draped on the sofa.

MUD & CHARTREUSE

An oversized shagreen-embossed leather ottoman supports an ebonized tray that allies with the dark wood table. The deep khaki-mud colour that Jamie Drake has used for the walls carries through to the lacquer of the built-in cupboards. Strong chartreuse touches make a style statement and lift the dark tones. Pewter glazed vases and antique silver bowls actively reflect the colours.

ESPRESSO & CREAM

This sofa has been upholstered in a great linen fabric called Mistral and the colour is fig. This shade is rich and redolent of autumn and is a marvellous neutral colour to use – without being at all predictable or boring. Bernie de le Cuona has accented it with desert-white pin-tucked linen cushions, as well as chocolate Madeline suede. The throw looks like a cross between fur, chenille and velvet and is called 'chinchilla' – perfect for a winter throw.

Paint colours

Off-whites

SNOW TO RICE PUDDING (PAGE 16)

Milk Benjamin Moore Simply White OC-117; Francesca's Paints Panna Cotta; Sherwin Williams White Flower SW 7102
Egg White Benjamin Moore Cotton Balls OC-122; Paint Library Paper I; Sherwin Williams Ibis White SW 7000
Rice Pudding Francesca's Paints Sand I; Paint Library Shell I
Snow Benjamin Moore Snowfall White OC-118; Fired Earth Oyster 31; Paint Library Sand I; Sherwin Williams Paper White SW 7105
Cream Soda Benjamin Moore Lemon Chiffon OC-109; Paint Library Oak I; Sherwin Williams Honied White SW 7106
Muslin Benjamin Moore White Diamond OC-61; Flamant 131 Cotton Grey; Sherwin Williams Futon SW 7101
Meringue Francesca's Paints Galao I; Sherwin Williams Pinkish SW 7112

BUTTER TO BISCUIT (PAGE 24)

Butter Benjamin Moore White Chocolate OC 127; Francesca's Paints Beachwood; Kelly Hoppen Clotted Cream; Sherwin Williams Downy SW 7002
Antique Lace Benjamin Moore Antique Yellow OC-103; Francesca's Paints Banana Smoothie; Paint Library Straw II
Vanilla Benjamin Moore Cream Silk OC-115; Francesca's Paints Boiled Egg II; Sherwin Williams Lily SW 6693
Beeswax Benjamin Moore Antiquity OC-107; Farrow & Ball New White 59; Sherwin Williams Morning Sun SW 6672
Clotted Cream Benjamin Moore Milkyway OC-110; Paint Library Ivory II; Sherwin Williams Venetian Lace SW 7119
Shortbread Benjamin Moore Timid White OC-39; Fired Earth Flake White 14; Sherwin Williams Dover white SW 6385
Biscuit Benjamin Moore Palace White OC-100; Francesca's Paints Galeo II; Kelly Hoppen Thai Beige; Paint Library Leather II; Sherwin Williams Reliable White SW 6091

OATMEAL TO TWINE (PAGE 31)

Calico Benjamin Moore Ancient Ivory OC-133; Flamant P03 Vanille; Sherwin Williams Dollop of Cream SW 7120
String Benjamin Moore Winter White OC-21; Flamant 119 Cool Ashes; Sherwin Williams Heron Plume SW 6070
Linen Benjamin Moore Soft Chamois OC-13; Kelly Hoppen Bone; Sherwin Williams Pearly White SW 7009
Twine Benjamin Moore Tapestry Beige OC-32; Kelly Hoppen Taupe; Sherwin Williams Popular Gray SW 6071
Oatmeal Benjamin Moore Moonlight White OC-125; Flamant 106 Old Church White; Francesca's Paints Peace White; Sherwin Williams Creamy SW 7012
Almond Benjamin Moore Spanish White OC-35; Farrow & Ball House White 2012; Sherwin Williams Cotton White SW 7104
Stone Benjamin Moore Morning Dew OC-140; Farrow & Ball Clunch 2009; Flamant 116 Bone; Sherwin Williams Natural Choice SW 7011

Greys

SILVER TO MIST (PAGE 44)

Ice Cube Benjamin Moore Mineral Ice 2132-70; Farrow & Ball Slipper Satin 2004; Sherwin Williams Original White SW 7077
Silver Francesca's Paints Elephant I; Sherwin Williams Eider White SW 7014
Venetian Marble Benjamin Moore Ice Cube Silver 2121-50; Francesca's Paints Elephant II; Sherwin Williams White Iris SW 6812

Sea Foam Benjamin Moore Gray Cloud 2126-60; Farrow & Ball James White 2010; Sherwin Williams Nebulous White SW 7063
Pearl Benjamin Moore Marilyn's Dress 2125-60; Francesca's Paints White Truffle; Sherwin Williams Discreet White SW 6266
Oyster Benjamin Moore Bunny Gray 2124-50; Francesca's Paints French Grey; Sherwin Williams Aura White SW 6532
Mist Benjamin Moore White Water 2120-60; Farrow & Ball Cornforth White 228; Francesca's Paints Peace White; Sherwin Williams Grayish SW 6001

DRIFTWOOD TO ELEPHANT (PAGE 54)

Abalone Benjamin Moore Pigeon Gray 2133-50; Crown RIBA Drawings Collection Neoclassical 8; Sherwin Williams Imagine SW 6009
Seal Benjamin Moore Shadow Gray 2125-40; Flamant SE322 Smoke; Sherwin Williams Network Gray SW 7073
Brushed Aluminium Benjamin Moore Silver Lining 2119-60; Fired Earth Pearl Ashes 3; Sherwin Williams North Star SW 6246
Driftwood Benjamin Moore White Stone 2134-60; Fired Earth Platinum Pale 2; Sherwin Williams Gray Screen SW 7071
Pewter Benjamin Moore Pewter 2121-30; Flamant P19 After Rain; Sherwin Williams Gray Matters SW 7066
Elephant Benjamin Moore Wolf Gray 2127-40; Farrow & Ball Mouse's Back 40; Flamant P14 Taupe; Francesca's Paints Havana Brown; Kelly Hoppen Nirvana; Sherwin Williams Sensuous Gray SW 7089
Grey Flannel Benjamin Moore Gray Timber Wolf 2126-50; Crown RIBA Drawings Collection Paladian 13; Sherwin Williams Quest Gray SW 7080; Flamant SE332 Atlantic

SHADOW TO EBONY (PAGE 63)

Shadow Benjamin Moore Smoke 2120-40; Crown RIBA Drawings Collection 50s Sketchbook 15; Kelly Hoppen Andaman Sea
Anthracite Benjamin Moore Gray 2121-10; Crown RIBA Drawings Collection Art Deco 15; Fired Earth Mercury 12
Ebony Benjamin Moore Twilight Zone 2127-10; Fired Earth Charcoal 6; Kelly Hoppen Ancient Black
Charcoal Benjamin Moore Almost Black 2130-30; Francesca's Paints Coopers Creek
Slate Benjamin Moore Anchor Gray 2126-30; Farrow & Ball Down Pipe 26; Flamant P31 Grey Flanel; Paint Library Squid Ink
Storm Cloud Benjamin Moore Gray Shower 2125-30; Flamant P29 Pavés du Nord; Sherwin Williams SW 6257 Gibraltar
Granite Benjamin Moore Black Horizon 2132-30; Farrow & Ball Off-black 57

Greens

CELADON TO PISTACHIO (PAGE 75)

Mint Granita Benjamin Moore Country Green 1B-540; Francesca's Paints Mint II; Sherwin Williams Lime Granita SW 6715
Celadon Benjamin Moore Dark Wren 2146-60; Flamant 171 Thé Vert; Francesca's Paints Mint I
Key Lime Pie Benjamin Moore Potpourri Green 2029-50; Crown Wind Chime Solo; Crown RIBA Drawings Collection 50s Sketchbook II; Dulux Willow Tree
Daiquiri Benjamin Moore Daiquiri Ice 2034-70; Francesca's Paints Minty Green; Paint Library Glass I; Sherwin Williams Spinach White SW 6434
Fennel Benjamin Moore Landscape 2B-430; Fired Earth Celadon
Pistachio Benjamin Moore Stem Green 2029-40; Crown RIBA Drawings Collection Arts and Crafts 4; Dulux Putting Green; Sherwin Williams Dancing Green SW 6716
Celery Benjamin Moore Pale Vista 2029-60; Paint Library Buttermint; Sherwin Williams Sprout SW 6427

LETTUCE TO JADE (PAGE 80)

Jade Francesca's Paints Lucia's Apple Green; Dulux Wild Forest; Paint Library Apple Smiles; Sherwin Williams Garden Grove SW 6445
Lettuce Benjamin Moore Potpourri Green 2029-50; Paint Library Pale Georgian; Sherwin Williams Baize Green SW 6429
Leaf Benjamin Moore Rosemary Green 2029-30; Paint Library Final Furlong; Sherwin Williams Overt Green SW 6718
Pear Benjamin Moore Kittery Paint Green HC-119; Crown RIBA Drawings Collection Neoclassical 15; Paint Library Stalk IV; Sherwin Williams Bonsai Tint SW 6436
Guacamole Benjamin Moore Pear Green 2028-40; Paint Library Euphorbia; Sherwin Williams Hearts of Palm SW 6472
Pea Soup Francesca's Paints Dew; Crown RIBA Drawings Collection 50s Sketchbook I; Paint Library Willow IV; Sherwin Williams Shagreen SW 6422
Winter Sea Benjamin Moore Winterberry Green HC-136; Francesca's Paints Federal Green; Sherwin Williams Composed SW 6472

GREEN TEA TO TOBACCO (PAGE 86)

Green Tea Benjamin Moore Brookside Moss 2145-30; Farrow & Ball Lichen 19; Flamant SE309 Pastis; Francesca's Paints Green Olive; Sherwin Williams Ryegrass SW 6423
Sage Benjamin Moore Kennebunkport Green HC-123; Francesca's Paints Classic Pesto; Paint Library Samphire; Sherwin Williams Artichoke SW 6179
Fig Benjamin Moore Herb Garden 4B-434; Farrow & Ball Calke Green 34; Sherwin Williams Inverness SW 6433
Olive Benjamin Moore Eucalyptus Leaf 2144-20; Farrow & Ball Olive 13; Flamant P75 Olive; Francesca's Paints Green Olive; Sherwin Williams Sheraton Sage SW 0014
Moss Benjamin Moore Webster Green HC-130; Fired Earth Zangar Green 108; Flamant P77 Vert Verger; Sherwin Williams Jadite SW 6459
Thyme Benjamin Moore Rosemary Sprig 2144-30; Paint Library Fowler's Olive; Sherwin Williams Tansy Green SW 6424
Tobacco Benjamin Moore Guacamole 2144-10; Fired Earth Wild Olive 120; Sherwin Williams Saguaro SW 6419

Blues

DUCK EGG TO DENIM (PAGE 97)

Duck Egg Benjamin Moore Glacier Blue 1B-1653; Crown RIBA Drawings Collection 50s Sketchbook II; Francesca's Paints Water Green II; Paint Library Ice IV; Sherwin Williams Atmosphere SW 6505
Wedgwood Benjamin Moore Blue Marguerite 2063-50; Crown RIBA Drawings Collection Victorian Eclectic 14; Sherwin Williams Resolute Blue SW 6507
Sky Benjamin Moore Swiss Blue 1B-815; Fired Earth Zenith Blue 88; Francesca's Paints Spanish Blue; Sherwin Williams Celestial SW 6808
Denim Benjamin Moore Water Town 3B-818; Crown RIBA Drawings Collection Victorian Eclectic 13; Flamant SE308 Myrtylle; Sherwin Williams Lupine SW 6810
Acquamarine Benjamin Moore Crisp Morning Air 1B-780; Farrow & Ball Duck Egg 99
Bluebell Benjamin Moore Jet Stream 1B-814; Francesca's Paints Salt Lake II; Paint Library Chalcedony; Sherwin Williams Wondrous Blue SW 6807
Light Teal Benjamin Moore Marlboro Blue HC-153; Flamant P86 Bleu Cap Ferrat; Francesca's Paints Salt Lake III; Sherwin Williams Open Seas SW 6500

LILAC TO HEATHER (PAGE 103)

Forget-me-not Benjamin Moore Victorian Trim 2068-60; Crown Dewberry Frost; Sherwin Williams Awesome Violet SW 6815
Lilac Benjamin Moore Lily Lavender 2071-60; Francesca's Paints Lilac; Paint Library Subtle Angel; Sherwin Williams Potentially Purple SW 6821
Hyacinth Benjamin Moore California Lilac 2068-40; Crown Mid Blue U7.24.48; Sherwin Williams Gentian SW 6817; B&Q Tate Range Pool
Wisteria Benjamin Moore Wishing Well 2B-1389; Flamant 158 Clic-Clac; Francesca's Paints Lavender III; Sherwin Williams Magical SW 6829
Thistle Benjamin Moore Spring Purple 2070-40; Fired Earth Gentian Violet 82; Sherwin Williams Dahlia SW 6816
Lavender Benjamin Moore Enchanted 2070-50; Flamant SE303 Glycine; Sherwin Williams Ash Violet SW 6549
Heather Benjamin Moore Purple Lotus 2072-30; Flamant 163 Venise; Francesca's Paints Piedmontese Aubergine; Sherwin Williams Plummy SW 6558

VIOLET TO MIDNIGHT (PAGE 110)

Indigo Benjamin Moore Scandinavian Blue 2068-30; Crown Peacock Blue; Francesca's Paints Royal Blue; Sherwin Williams Morning Glory SW 6971
Peacock Benjamin Moore Blue Danube 2062-30; Crown Dark Grey P9.26.35; Flamant 150 Les Flots Bleus; Sherwin Williams Georgian Bay SW 6509
Violet Benjamin Moore Mystical Grape 2071-30; Dulux Soft Aubergine; Sherwin Williams African Violet SW 6982
Deep Teal Benjamin Moore Bermuda Blue 2061-30; Crown RIBA Drawings Collection Arts and Crafts 12; Sherwin Williams Bosporus SW 6503
Midnight Benjamin Moore Midnight Navy 2067-10; Crown Dramatic; Sherwin Williams Dignified SW 6538
Cobalt Blue Benjamin Moore Champion Cobalt 2061-20; Dulux Niagra Blues; Paint Library Blue Blood; Sherwin Williams Regatta SW 6517
Petrol Benjamin Moore Down Pour Blue 2063-20; Crown RIBA Drawings Collection Gothic Revival 15; Sherwin Williams Dignity Blue SW 6804

Pinks

CHERRY BLOSSOM TO FUCHSIA (PAGE 120)

Cherry Blossom Crown RIBA Drawings Collection Neoclassical 6; Francesca's Paints Rose I; Paint Library Oyster Lily; Sherwin Williams Amour Pink SW 6595
Watermelon Benjamin Moore Wild Pink 2080-40; Crown Pagoda; Sherwin Williams Cyclamen SW 6571
Strawberry Mousse Crown Mademoiselle; Francesca's Paints Rose II; Sherwin Williams Lighthearted Pink SW 6568
Fuchsia Benjamin Moore Peony 2079-30; Crown Shocking Pink; Francesca's Paints Pigi's Piggy Pink
Sweet Pea Benjamin Moore Bunny Nose Pink 2074-60; Crown Beauty Queen; Francesca's Paints Rose III; Sherwin Williams Vanity Pink SW 6976
Rose Benjamin Moore Paradise Pink 2078-40; Francesca's Paints Rose Bank; Sherwin Williams Vivacious Pink SW 6850
Raspberry Fool Benjamin Moore Pink Begonia 2078-50; Sherwin Williams Partytime SW 6849

CRANBERRY TO RHUBARB (PAGE 127)

Rhubarb Benjamin Moore Vibrant Blush 2081-30; Crown Dawn Grey A8.25.48; Crown Summer Pudding; Francesca's Paints Rose; Sherwin Williams Heartfelt SW 6586;
Poppy Benjamin Moore Spring Tulips 2001-30; Crown Russet C4.60.40; Crown Scooter Red; Sherwin Williams Stop SW 6869
Cherry Benjamin Moore Candy Cane Red 2079-10; Dulux Windsor Red; Sherwin Williams Radish SW 6861

Summer Pudding Benjamin Moore Rose Parade 2086-20; Fired Earth Bengal Rose; Sherwin Williams Cherries Jubilee SW 6862
Cranberry Benjamin Moore Blushing Red 2079-20; Crown Bright Red C4.60.30; Sherwin Williams Gala Pink SW 6579
Sangria Benjamin Moore Raspberry Glaze 2078-20; Flamant HC157 Lipstick; Sherwin Williams Hot SW 6843
Strawberry Benjamin Moore Exotic Red 2086-10; Flamant HC156 Rouge Baiser; Sherwin Williams Positive Red SW 6871

CLARET TO AUBERGINE (PAGE 132)

Claret Benjamin Moore Crushed Velvet 2076-10; Farrow & Ball Rectory Red 217; Paint Library Elisabethan Red; Sherwin Williams Valentine SW 6587
Aubergine Benjamin Moore Dark Burgundy 2075-10; Crown Burgundy; Flamant SE304 Grand Cru; Sherwin Williams Burgundy SW 6300
Beetroot Benjamin Moore Magenta 2077-10; Dulux Heritage Collection Pugin Red; Sherwin Williams Forward Fuchsia SW 6842
Plum Benjamin Moore Roseate 2078-10; Flamant SE305 Castille; Kelly Hoppen Chinese Red; Sherwin Williams Cerise SW 6580
Mulberry Benjamin Moore Mulberry 2075-20; Francesca's Paints Jacaranda; Kelly Hoppen Red Lantern; Sherwin Williams Fabulous Grape SW 6293
Blackberry Benjamin Moore Autumn Purple 2073-20; Kelly Hoppen Opium Den; Sherwin Williams Kimono Violet SW 6839
Grape Juice Crown Bright Red; A1.36.22; Sherwin Williams Juneberry SW 6573

Sunny tones

SAND TO OCHRE (PAGE 142)

Saffron Dulux Soft Solar; Francesca's Paints Neisha Crosland I Yellow Chalk; Paint Library Othman Brae; Sherwin Williams Bee SW 6683
Ochre Benjamin Moore Cork 2153-40; Farrow & Ball Cane 53; Flamant P60 Dunes; Paint Library Cloudberry; Sherwin Williams Golden Fleece SW 6388
Maize Benjamin Moore Suntan Yellow 2155-50; Francesca's Paints Tobacco; Sherwin Williams Jonquil SW 6674
Sand Benjamin Moore Golden Straw 2152-50; Farrow & Ball Farrow's Cream 67; Francesca's Paints Mascarpone; Sherwin Williams Inviting Ivory SW 6372
Peach Sorbet Benjamin Moore Asbury Sand 2156-50; Farrow & Ball Yellow Ground 218; Francesca's Paints Morocco; Sherwin Williams Honey Blush SW 6660
Sunflower Crown RIBA Drawings Collection Victorian Eclectic 4; Francesca's Paints Yellow Peppers; Sherwin Williams Butterfield SW 6676
Hay Farrow & Ball Dorset Cream 68; Francesca's Paints Galao III; Sherwin Williams Interactive Cream SW 6113

TOPAZ TO TERRACOTTA (PAGE 149)

Paprika Francesca's Paints Barbara's Pink; Flamant P38 Sienna; Sherwin Williams Henna Shade SW 6326
Chilli Pepper Francesca's Paints Rebecca's Red; Farrow & Ball Blazer 212; Sherwin Williams Reddish SW 6319
Topaz Francesca's Paints Arabella's Pumpkin; Flamant SE319 Tango; Sherwin Williams Outgoing Orange SW 6641
Tuscan Wall Francesca's Paints Gioia's Madras; Crown RIBA Drawings Collection 50s Sketchbook 6; Dulux Tuscan Terracotta; Sherwin Williams Persimmon SW 6339
Burnt Sienna Benjamin Moore Rust 2175-30; Farrow & Ball Red Earth 64; Sherwin Williams Reynard SW 6348
Tomato Salsa Benjamin Moore Adobe Orange 2171-30; Crown RIBA Drawings Collection 50s Sketchbook 9; Sherwin Williams Obstinate Orange SW 6884
Terracotta Benjamin Moore Terra Cotta Tile 2090-30;

Flamant P42 Briques de Bruges; Francesca's Paints Marco's Terracotta; Sherwin Williams Spicy Hue SW 6324

Earth & spice

CAMEL TO MOLE (PAGE 160)

Camel Benjamin Moore Chestertown Buff HC-9; Francesco's Paints Alessandro's Caramel; Kelly Hoppen Basket; Sherwin Williams Restrained Gold SW 6129
Brown Bread Benjamin Moore Sag Harbour Gray HC-95; Crown RIBA Drawings Collection Art Deco 8; Flamant P11 Bord de Seine; Kelly Hoppen Taupe on Tap; Sherwin Williams Sand Trap SW 6066
Malted Milk Benjamin Moore Bradstreet Beige HC-48; Francesca's Paints Petal; Kelly Hoppen Incense; Sherwin Williams Malted Milk SW 6057
Praline Truffle Benjamin Moore Sandlot Gray 2107-50; Kelly Hoppen Zen; Sherwin Williams Doeskin SW 6064
Latte Francesca's Paints Sand III; Francesca's Paints Gianluca's Fawn; Kelly Hoppen Pebble; Sherwin Williams Basket Beige SW 6143
Mole Benjamin Moore Stardust 2108-40; Kelly Hoppen Nirvana; Sherwin Williams Poised Taupe SW 6039
Mushroom Benjamin Moore Shenandoah Taupe HC-36; Farrow & Ball Dead Salmon 28; Sherwin Williams Glamour SW 6031

GINGER TO CINNAMON (PAGE 167)

Cognac Benjamin Moore Richmond Gold HC-41; Flamant P36 Savane; Sherwin Williams Tatami Tan SW 6116
Mocha Benjamin Moore Mudslide 2095-40; Crown RIBA Drawings Collection Revival 7; Francesca's Paints Dune 45 II; Sherwin Williams Reddened Earth SW 6053
Muscovado Sugar Benjamin Moore Peanut Shell 2162-40; Flamant P33 Terre de Picardie; Francesca's Paints Dune 45 I; Sherwin Williams Bagel SW 6114
Cinnamon Benjamin Moore Rich Clay Brown 2164-30; Francesca's Paints Pump Room Red; Sherwin Williams Canyon Clay SW 6054
Caramel Benjamin Moore Roxbury Caramel HC-42; Flamant P34 Dalle Industrielle; Francesca's Paints Spitzkop II; Sherwin Williams Totally Tan SW 6115
Ginger Benjamin Moore Dark Mustard 2161-30; Crown RIBA Drawings Collection Victorian Eclectic 5; Sherwin Williams Decorous Amber SW 0007
French Mustard Benjamin Moore Tyler Taupe HC-43; Crown RIBA Drawings Collection Regency 5; Francesca's Paints Etosha II; Sherwin Williams Baguette SW 6123

TOFFEE TO CHOCOLATE (PAGE 172)

Gingerbread Benjamin Moore Cocoa Brown 2101-20; Crown RIBA Drawings Collection Gothic Revival 10; Farrow & Ball Etruscan Red 56; Paint Library Hopsack; Sherwin Williams Aurora Brown SW 2837
Chocolate Benjamin Moore Mocha Brown 2107-20; Crown Chestnut; Dulux Chocolate Fondant; Paint Library Masai; Sherwin Williams Fiery Brown SW 6055
Toffee Benjamin Moore Greenfield Pumpkin HC-40; Flamant P62 Indian Summer; Sherwin Williams Renwick Rose Beige SW 2804
Molasses Benjamin Moore Cinnamon Slate 2113-40; Farrow & Ball Dauphin 54; Fired Earth Scarab 42; Flamant SE318 Coco; Sherwin Williams Tanbark SW 6061
Saddle Brown Benjamin Moore Grandfather Clock Brown 2096-30; Fired Earth Pompeiian Red 69; Francesca's Paints Mud; Sherwin Williams Moroccan Brown SW 6060
Rye Bread Benjamin Moore Brown Horse 2108-30; Farrow & Ball Wainscot 55; Fired Earth Raw Earth 17; Sherwin Williams Rookwood Dark Brown SW 2808
Coffee Beans Benjamin Moore Grizzly Bear Brown 2111-20; Fired Earth Sepia 18; Sherwin Williams French Roast SW 6069

Swatches

Off-whites

SNOW TO RICE PUDDING (PAGE 23)

Fabric

1 Sun Atelier, SF-EMB-006/02
2 De le Cuona, Linen Shade Ivory, KKK2
3 Chase Erwin, Hampton Check, Chocolate
5 De le Cuona, 100% Cashmere
8 Sahco, Ulf Moritz, Elecaro, 1273-02
10 Abbott & Boyd Ltd, Code A, Jasmin de Nuit, 17080-02
11 Nina Campbell, Meryton Collection, Meryton, NCF3670/01, distributed by Osborne & Little
13 Andrew Martin, Cotton Petit, Beige/White
14 De le Cuona, Paper Bark All White, PA9

Flooring

4 Kersaint Cobb & Company, KC Pampas Braydale, 33620-11-173
6 Alternative Flooring Company, 4001 Leather Parchment (Edges)
7 Element 7, Washed Lunar Larch Lye
9 Crucial Trading, Wide Bamboo, Limewash, WB01
12 Limestone Gallery, Ivory Premium Gloss

BUTTER TO BISCUIT (PAGES 28–9)

Fabric

1 Andrew Martin, Georgia Collection, Washington Velvet, Pongee
3 De le Cuona, Storm Papyrus, NN1
4 Nina Campbell, Bovary Collection, Deauville, Ref. NCF3704/03
5 De le Cuona, Paper Bark Chalk, PA8
8 Sun Atelier, SF-EMB-111/01, Dupion Embroidery
9 Sun Atelier, SF-TF-CHK-002/01
11 Andrew Martin, Corduroy, Nutmeg
12 Kelly Hoppen, Cashmere, Incense/Black Pinstripe, KHI9202

Flooring

2 Adam, Quality: Natural Perceptions, Name: PL09 Lattice Olive
6 Element 7, Washed Fine Oak
7 Crucial Trading, Mississippi Stripe, Willow/Oatmeal, WS105
10 Walton Ceramics, W14, Rust Cream

OATMEAL TO TWINE (PAGE 37)

Fabric

1 Andrew Martin, Pullman Collection, Constantinople Cocoa
2 De le Cuona, Linen Shade Stone, KKK4
3 De le Cuona, Mutt Cloth Cream, AS2
4 De le Cuona, Rural Slate, S8
5 De le Cuona, 100% Cashmere
7 The Alternative Flooring Company, 4001 Parchment (Edges)
9 Chelsea textile, FC357 Large Check, Sand
11 De le Cuona, Shire Oatmeal, D1
12 De le Cuona, Mutt Stripe Cream, AT2
13 De le Cuona, Paper Bark Lime White, PA6

Flooring

6 Element 7, Fired Acacia
8 Adam Textures, Rustic Croft, Taransay, CR13
10 Walton Ceramics, Rust, W14

Greys

SILVER TO MIST (PAGE 53)

Fabric

1 Sun Atelier, SF-TF-STR-002/06
2 Chelsea Textiles, F2009 B, Pinneapple & Auricula, Blue
5 Andrew Martin, Georgia Collection, Congress, Alabaster
6 Chase Erwin, Sequin, Mist
7 Sahco Ulf Moritz, Cristallo, 2082-01
8 De le Cuona, Louiza Paisley, Mist, No. LO1
9 Sun Atelier, Pleated Fabric
11 Kelly Hoppen, Boiled Wool, Smoke, KHI5104
12 Sun Atelier, SF-Emb-008/04
13 Anya Larkin Ltd, Shagreen 2607 Hickory
14 Nina Campbell, Bovary Collection, Bovary, Ref. NCF3700/05

Flooring

3 Ebonyandco, Un-milled Original Surface Barnwood
4 Crucial Trading, Linton, Stone, WS500
10 Limestone Gallery, Ivory Nuage

DRIFTWOOD TO ELEPHANT (PAGE 61)

Fabric

1 Andrew Martin, Minstral Collection, Tumba, Storm
2 Sahco, Ulf Moritz, Elecaro, 1273-01
4 Edelman, All Grain, Burnt Orange, AG14
6 Andrew Martin, Brummel Plain, Gun Metal
7 Sun Atelier, SFD 229
8 Edelman, Real Woven, Black, RW02
9 Andrew Martin, Rama Collection, Varuna, Grey
11 Kelly Hoppen, Boiled Wool, Ash, KHI5105
13 Andrew Martin, Georgia Collection, Washington Velvet, Gargoyle
14 Andrew Martin, Prince of Wales Check
15 Andrew Martin, Sheers, 2608 120
16 De le Cuona, Kyoto Pewter, KY5
17 De le Cuona, Mutt Stripe Cream, AT2
18 De le Cuona, Sun Bleached Paisley Whisper, HH3

Flooring

3 Crucial Trading, Sisal, Panama Accents, Charcoal n Flint, E893
5 Limestone Gallery, 2729-St Michel
10 Crucial Trading, Chunky, Silver Birch, WF158
12 The Alternative Flooring Company, Sisal Bouclé, Bitterne, 1225

SHADOW TO EBONY (PAGE 69)

Fabric

1 De le Cuona, Mutt Cloth Black, AS1
2 Andrew Martin, Burford Collection, Burford, Charcoal
3 Designers Guild, F1166/02, Amboise-Raspberry
4 De le Cuona, 100% Cashmere
5 Kelly Hoppen, Cashmere, Ink, KHI9302
6 De le Cuona, Linen Shade Ivory, KKK2
7 Andrew Martin, Chalk Stripe, Charcoal
10 Andrew Martin, Rawhide, Crystal Black
11 Kravet, 21228, 81
13 Andrew Martin, Chaucer Collection, Chaucer Hand Block Velvet, Black
14 Andrew Martin, Havana, Nubia Black
15 Andrew Martin, Taynton Collection, Taynton, Pomelo
16 Andrew Martin, Ardecora, 18 5085 989
17 De le Cuona, Alexander Paisley, Red, BA1

Flooring

8 Crucial Trading, Linton, Charcoal, WS504
9 Ebonyandco, Select White Oak, 2 Enonyandco Stains
12 Brintons Carpets, Bell Twist, Smoke, 16082

Greens

CELADON TO PISTACHIO (PAGES 78–9)

Fabric

1 De le Cuona, Museum Cloth, Acorn, AE4
2 Chelsea Textiles, FCV715, Thin Stripe Seamist
3 Chelsea Textiles, F801, Green Embroidery on Coloured Hemp Ground
5 Chelsea Textiles, F204SW, Tulip – Upholstery Weight
7 Edelman, Shagreen, Sha-green, SH03
8 Sun Atelier, SF-CHK-001/01, Taffeta Checks
9 African Light Trading, Ostrich Leg, Lime
10 Nina Campbell, Cha Cha Weaves Collection, Quickstep, NCF3570/11
12 Chelsea Textiles, F160 William Morris Leaf
13 De le Cuona, Paper Bark Cooking Apple, PA4
14 Chelsea Textiles, 2009G, Pale Green

Flooring

4 Ebonyandco, Eastern White Pine, 2 Ebonyandco Stains
6 Limestone Gallery, Onix Green Dark, 2702
11 Brintons Carpets, Claude Sage, F424

LETTUCE TO JADE (PAGE 85)

Fabric

1 De le Cuona, Peasent Cloth Dew, AA6
2 Edelman, Old Rattlesnake, Waterfalls OLD-S5
3 Chelsea Textiles, FC281, Medium Check, Green
4 Travers, Hollyhock, Aubergine and Mint, 107015
5 Nina Campbell, Ptarmigan Weaves Collection, Partridge, NCF3614/04
6 Andrew Martin, Lundy, Samphire
10 Andrew Martin, Tricot – 09
11 De le Cuona, Antique Paisley, Blue
12 Chelsea Textiles, F199 WG, Sprigs and Leaves in White on Green

Flooring

7 Limestone Gallery, Jerusalem Blue Honed
8 Walton Ceramics, Porcelain Green Slate, W29
9 Element 7, Natural Fine Oak
13 Cormar Carpets, Warwick Collection, Fern

GREEN TEA TO TOBACCO (PAGE 91)

Fabric

1 Sun Atelier, SF-CHK-001/04, Taffeta Checks
2 Nina Campbell, Ptarmigan Weaves Collection, Partridge, NCF3614/05
3 Chelsea Textiles, FC104, Large Check, Green/Olive
4 Nina Campbell, Vaucluse Collection, Vaucluse Stripe, NCF3450/06, distributed by Osborne & Little
5 De le Cuona, Chinchilla Coconut, CH5
6 Andrew Martin, Stanway Collection, Stanway, Sage
8 Andrew Martin, Lundy, Khaki
9 Sun Atelier, SF-TF-STR-25C, Taffeta Stripes
10 De le Cuona, Paper Bark Frog, PA7
11 De le Cuona, Linen Shade Ivory, KKK2
12 Andrew Martin, Hidcote Collection, Panna Cotta Moss
13 Brunschwig & Fils, 79521-432
14 Nina Campbell, Vaucluse Collection, Vaucluse Plain, NCF3451/16, distributed by Osborne & Little

Flooring

7 Element 7, Fired Acacia

Blues

DUCK EGG TO DENIM (PAGE 101)

Fabric

1 De le Cuona, 100 % Cashmere
2 Nina Campbell, Vaucluse Collection, Vaucluse Stripe, NCF3450/04
3 De le Cuona, Ruffle Linen, Shade of Blue, AD4
6 Andrew Martin, Tricot, 13
8 De le Cuona, Sun Bleached Paisley, Cloud, HH1
10 Travers, Duchess, Sand, 100402
11 Travers, Duchess, Sky, 100426
12 Chelsea Textiles, 208B
13 Andrew Martin, Washington Velvet, Vanilla/131
14 Andrew Martin, Taynton Collection, Woodstock, Aero
15 Andrew Martin, Taynton Collection, Taynton, Fresh Blue

Flooring

4 Kersaint Cobb & Company, Moutain Grass, Herringbone

5 Element 7, Washed Lunar Larch Lye

7 Limestone Gallery, Limeira Honed

9 Kersaint Cobb & Company, KC Pampas Braydale, 33620-11-147

LILAC TO HEATHER (PAGES 108–9)

Fabric

1 De le Cuona, Scrunch Cloth Oyster White, BG1

2 Sun Atelier, SF-EMB-050/01

3 Andrew Martin, Academy, Anemone

4 De le Cuona, Ikat Purple, AM2

5 Nina Campbell, Twist Collection, Twist, NCF3580/14

6 De le Cuona, Silk Paisley, Heather, SP2

7 Osborne & Little, Taisho Silks Collection, Suji, F5483/02

10 Andrew Martin, Burford Collection, Bibury, Clover

11 Andrew Martin, Delta, Lion

12 De le Cuona, 100% Cashmere

14 Nina Cambpell, Fandango Stripes Collection, Rumba, NCF3602/02

15 Abbott & Boyd, Code A, Velours, 17039-05

16 Chelsea Textiles, FC352, Large Check, Mauve

Flooring

8 Element 7, Washed Fine Oak

9 The Alternative Flooring Company, Wool Dapple, Nougat, 1782

13 Limestone Gallery, 2707 Onyx Cammello

VIOLET TO MIDNIGHT (PAGE 115)

Fabric

1 De le Cuona, Regency Blackcurrant, AL2

2 De le Cuona, Colonial Blackcurrant, AN4

3 Andrew Martin, Washington Velvet, Deep Purple/310

4 Andrew Martin, Carnaval Collection, Rex, Blackcurrant

6 Nina Campbell, Ptarmigan Weaves Collection, Woodcock, NCF3611/02

7 Andrew Martin, Thackeray, Pergola, Delphinium

8 Chase Erwin, Admiral Check, Navy

9 Andrew Martin, Americana Collection, Indigo Plain

10 Andrew Martin, Discovery Collection, Kano, Blue

12 Andrew Martin, Achill, 111

13 Andrew Martin, Washington Velvet, Midnight/352

14 Chelsea Textile, Green Embroidery, F801

15 Edelman, Woven Leather, Licorice WVN7

Flooring

5 Walton Ceramics, Blue Azur, W14

11 Walton Ceramics, Palio Light Polished, W14

Pinks

CHERRY BLOSSOM TO FUCHSIA (PAGE 125)

Fabric

1 Sun Atelier, SF-TF-STR-ID

3 Chelsea Textiles, F2009 RA, Pineapple and Auricula in Red on a Dark Ground

4 Andrew Martin, Taynton Collection, Taynton, Pomelo

6 De le Cuona, Ocean Drive Sun, OD1

8 Andrew Martin, Burford Collection, Burford, Raspberry

9 Chelsea Textiles, FCV712, Narrow Stripe Raspberry Voile

10 De le Cuona, Portfolio Cherry, PO6

11 Sun Atelier, SF-EMB-108/01

Flooring

2 Cormar Carpets, Warwick Collection, Tigerlily

5 The Alternative Flooring Company, Wool Pebble, Portland, 1777

7 Limestone Gallery, 2504 Rosa Tea

CRANBERRY TO RHUBARB (PAGE 131)

Fabric

1 Edelman, Cavallini, Crimson C24

2 Osborne & Little, Collection: Zameen Silks, Tigre, Ref: F5351/01

4 De le Cuona, Hornbuckle, Red Earth, NN5

7 De le Cuona, Bandit Burgundy, TA1

10 Andrew Martin, Carnival Collection, Masquerade, Punch

11 Sun Atelier, Jute Embroidery

12 Edelman, Real Woven, Cherry Red, RW06

13 De le Cuona, Lodge Rouge, G5

14 Chelsea Textiles, F 054TR, Flowers in Tea on Red

15 De le Cuona, Coast Ruby, H2

16 De le Cuona, Lyon Stripe Wine, MMM4

Flooring

3 The Alternative Flooring Company, Sisal Herringbone, Hockley, 4422

5 Ebonyandco, White Oak, 2 Ebonyandco Stains

6 Crucial Trading, Linen Basketweave, LB18 Tomato (Edges)

8 The Alternative Flooring Company, Sisal Herringbone, Hampton, 4420

9 Limestone Gallery, 2502 Crema Valencia Gloss

CLARET TO AUBERGINE (PAGES 136–7)

Fabric

1 Ardecora, Aragon 18 10014 394

2 Osborne & Little, Taisho Silks Collection, Kado, F5482/06

4 Nina Campbell, Contarini Collection, Contarini Stripe, NCF3501/02

5 Andrew Martin, Carnival Collection, Masquerade, Eggplant

6 De le Cuona, Storm Papyrus, NN1

8 Abbott & Boyd Ltd, Code A, Taffetas Plisse, 17058-9

9 Andrew Martin, Washington Velvet, Wine/8

10 Trade Routes, Ostrich, Bordeaux

11 Zimmer + Rohde, 18 6023 347

12 Chase Erwin, Elixir, Burgundy

13 Kravet, 21363-816

15 De le Cuona, 100% Cashmere

Flooring

3 Limestone Gallery, 2733 Rosso Lepanto Gloss

7 Element 7, Washed Fine Oak

14 GMS Stone Floors, Riverbed Flagstones

Sunny tones

SAND TO OCHRE (PAGE 147)

Fabric

4 Edelman, All Grain, Baked Bean AG06

5 Chelsea Textiles, F804

6 Nina Campbell, Contarini Collection, Contarini Stripe, NCF3501/04

7 Kravet, 21233, 816

8 Trade Routes, Ostrich, Oryx

9 Andrew Martin, Georgia Collection, Congress, Sandcastle

10 Sun Atelier, SF-TF-STR-002/02, 9-inch Taffeta Stripes

11 Boussac, Santiago, 7683, 02 Beige

14 Andrew Martin, Burford Collection, Burford, Cream

Flooring

1 Adam Textures, TW2, Wattle Corn

2 Ebonyandco, White Oak, 1 Cherry Stain, Tung Oil Topcoat

3 Crucial Trading, Mississippi Stripe, Orange/Gold, WS104

12 Limestone Gallery, Jerusalem Raliu

13 Crucial Trading, Linen Basketweave, LB19 Sand (Edges)

TOPAZ TO TERRACOTTA (PAGE 155)

Fabric

1 Edelman, Royal Suede, Paprika, RS43

2 De le Cuona, Louiza Paisley, Coral, LO4

4 Andrew Martin, Naivasha Collection, Mombasa, Rust

5 Osborne & Little, Taisho Silks Collection, Suji, F5483/01

7 Sun Atelier, SF-TF-STR-25B, Taffeta Stripes

9 Sahco, Ulf Moritz, Tamarinda, 2055-08

12 African Light Trading, Ostrich, Copper

13 De le Cuona, Rainier Paisley, Coral, MMM1

14 Andrew Martin, Petrov, Coral

Flooring

3 The Alternative Flooring Company, Sisal Panama, Russet Red, 2524

6 Adam, Kasbah Twist, KT34 Kashmir

8 Walton Ceramics, Craftsmanship, W38

10 Crucial Trading, Bamboo, Copper, WB03

11 Crucial Trading, Cotton Herringbone, C25 Ketchup (Edges)

Earth tones

CAMEL TO MOLE (PAGE 165)

Fabric

1 Chase Erwin, Ultrasuede, Beaver, 3274

2 Sun Atelier, SFT-03, Silk Taffeta

4 Kravet, 21365-816

5 Nina Campbell, Contarini Collection, Contarini Stripe, NCF3501/06

6 De le Cuona, 100% Cashmere

8 Travers, 402651, Rousseau Velvet Square, Chestnut

10 Kelly Hoppen, Cashmere, KHI9205, Saddle

11 Sun Atelier, SF-TF-STR-002/01

12 Andrew Martin, Limpopo, Emu Dark Brown

14 De le Cuona, Shire Wood, D3

Flooring

3 Kersaint Cobb & Company, KC Linen, 785/16

7 The Alternative Flooring Company, Wool Sisal Mix, Bergamot, 1653

9 Limestone Gallery, Emperador Light

13 Brintons Carpets, Bell Twist, Wheatsheaf B42

GINGER TO CINNAMON (PAGE 171)

Fabric

2 Chelsea Textiles, F803, Dots and Circles

3 Travers, Delauney Silk Velvet, Sienna, 401732

4 De le Cuona, Chinchilla Almond, CH4

5 Edelman, All Grain, Baked Bean, AG06

6 Travers, Hollyhock, Aubergine & Mint, 107015

9 Andrew Martin, Sheers II, 10039 848

10 Andrew Martin, Rawhide, Antiqued Hide

11 Kravet, 21229-816

12 Nina Campbell, Ptarmigan Weaves Collection, Partridge, NCF3614/01

Flooring

1 Crucial Trading, Mississippi Stripe, Coffee/Cream, WS106

7 Limestone Gallery, 2506 Rojo Alicante

8 Crucial Trading, Wide Bamboo, Natural, WB02

13 The Alternative Flooring Company, Sisal Bouclé, Red Natural, 1203

TOFFEE TO CHOCOLATE (PAGES 178–8)

Fabric

1 Chase Erwin, Rib, Truffle

2 De le Cuona, 100% Cashmere

3 Andrew Martin, Limpopo, Bison

4 Andrew Martin, Georgia Collection, Congress, Slate

7 Kravet, 21366-816

8 De le Cuona, Shire Wood

9 Andrew Martin, Limpopo, Mkuzi Dark Brown

11 Andrew Martin, Pushkin, Coffee

12 Designers Guild, F1245/01, Spinelli Cocoa

13 Andrew Martin, Painswick Collection, Painswick, Chocolate

14 Sun Atelier, SFT-06

15 Andrew Martin, Parasol, Charcoal

16 Andrew Martin, Rawhide, Rhino Black

Flooring

5 Element 7, Nero Oak

6 The Alternative Flooring Company, Sisal Bouclé, Blue Natural, 1205

10 Crucial Trading, Mahon, Oatmeal, WM311

Sources

PAINT

Benjamin Moore
+1 800 344 0400
www.benjaminmoore.com

Cole & Son
+44 (0)20 7376 4628
www.cole-and-son.com

Color Wheel Paints
+1 407 293 6810
+1 800 749 6810
www.colorwheelpaint.com

Crown Paint
+44 (0)870 240 1127
www.crownpaint.co.uk

Dulux
+44 (0)870 444 1111
www.dulux.co.uk

Emery & Cie
+32 2 534 4770
+1 718 767 8218
www.emeryetcie.com

Farrow & Ball
+44 (0)1202 876 141
+1 888 511 1121
www.farrow-ball.com

Fine Paints of Europe
+1 800 332 1556
www.finepaintsofeurope.com

Fired Earth
+44 (0)1295 812 088
www.firedearth.com

Flamant
+32 (0)474 97 58 86
www.flamantpaint.com
distributed in London by
Ma Maison

Francesca's Paint Ltd
+44 (0)20 7228 7694
www.francescaspaint.com

Hammerite
+44 (0)870 444 1111
www.hammerite.com

Harris
+44 (0)1527 575 441
+44 (0)800 136 982
www.lgharris.co.uk

Heritage paints
+44 (0)1753 550 555
www.heritagepaints.co.uk

Kelly Hoppen Paints
+44 (0)20 7471 3350
www.kellyhoppen.com

Leyland Paint
+44 (0)1924 354 000
www.leyland-paints.co.uk

The Little Greene
+44 (0)161 230 0880
www.thelittlegreene.com

Marston & Langinger
+44 (0)20 7881 5783
+1 212 965 0434
www.marston-and-
langinger.com

Martha Stewart
+1 888 5 MARTHA
www.marthastewart.com

Paint & Paper Library
+44 (0)20 7823 7755
www.paintlibrary.co.uk

Paper & Paints
+44 (0)20 7352 8626

Plascon
+44 (0)860 204 060
www.plascon.co.za

Ralph Lauren Paint
+1 800 379 POLO
www.rlhome.polo.com

Ressource
+33 (0)1 42 22 58 80

Sherwin-Williams
www.sherwin-williams.com

**Sydney Harbour Paint
Company**
www.sydneyharbourpaints.com
+1 877 228 8440

WALLPAPER

Anya Larkin
+1 212 532 3263
www.anyalarkin.com

The Art of Wallpaper
+44 (0)1508 531 171
www.theartofwallpaper.com

Borderline
+44 (0)20 7823 3567
www.borderlinefabrics.com

**Churchill Fabrics and
Wallpapers**
+44 (0)20 7244 7427
www.janechurchill.com

De Gournay
+44 (0)20 7823 7316
+1 212 564 9750
www.degournay.com

Elizabeth Dow Ltd
+1 631 267 3401
www.elizabethdow.com

Graham & Brown
+1 800 554 0887
www.grahambrown.com

Muraspec
+44 (0)8705 117 118
www.muraspec.com

Nobilis
+33 (0)1 43 29 21 50
+44 (0)20 8767 0774
www.nobilis.fr

Philip Jeffries
+1 800 576 5455
www.phillipjeffries.com

Sandberg
+46 (0)321 531 660
www.sandbergtapeter.se

William Yeoward
+44 (0)20 7349 7828
www.williamyeoward.com

CARPET

Adam Carpet
+44 (0)1562 822 247
www.carpetinfo.co.uk

**The Alternative Flooring
Company**
+44 (0)1264 335 111
www.alternativeflooring.com

Blenheim Carpets
+44 (0)20 7823 6333
www.blenheim-carpets.com

Brintons Carpet
+44 (0)1562 635 665
+44 (0)800 505 055
www.brintons.net

Cavalier Carpets
+ 44 (0)1254 268 000
www.cavaliercarpets.co.uk

Cormar Carpets
www.cormarcarpets.co.uk

Crucial Trading
+44 (0)1562 743 747
www.crucial-trading.com

Doris Leslie Blau
+1 212 586 5511
(antique carpets)
+1 212 752 7623 (custom
carpets/decorative arts)
www.dorisleslieblau.com

Fort Street Studio
+44 (0)20 7589 5946
+1 212 925 5383
www.fortstreetstudio.com

Kersaint Cobb & Cie
+44 (0)1675 430 430
www.kersaintcobb.co.uk

Merida Meridian
+1 617 464 5400
+1 800 345 2200
www.meridameridian.com

The Rug Company
+44 (0)20 7229 5148
+1 212 274 0444
www.therugcompany.info

STONE/TILE FLOORS
AND SURFACES

Ann Sacks
+1 800 278 TILE
www.annsacks.com

Corian Solid Surfaces
+44 (0)800 962 116
+1 800 906 7765
www.corian.com

GMI Stone
+44 (0)20 7498 2742

Granite & Marble
+1 718 832 3628

Granite Marble & Stone Ltd
+44 (0)1580 212 222
www.naturalstonefloors.org

Keysgranite
1 305 477 7363
+ 800 8 GRANITE
www.keysgranite.com

Limestone Gallery
+44 (0)20 7735 8555
www.limestonegallery.com

Marmi & Granito
+44 (0)20 7622 0438
www.marmi.co.uk

Paris ceramics
+1 212 644 2782
www.parisceramics.com

Tiles & Stones
+1 305 718 8133
www.tilesandstones.com

Unimar Ltd
+44 (0)20 8810 7788
www.unimarltd.co.uk

Walker Zanger
+1 818 252 4005
www.walkerzanger.com

Walton Ceramics
+44 (0)20 7589 7386
www.waltonceramics.co.uk

WOOD FLOORS

Ebony & Co
+44 (0)20 7259 0000
+1 212 426 7505
www.ebonyandco.com

Element 7
+44 (0)20 7736 2366
www.element7.co.uk

Floors 2 Go
+44 (0)800 830 330
www.floors2go.co.uk

Junckers
+44 (0)1376 534 700
+44 (0)845 230 9885
www.junckers.com

Mafkildea
+44 (0)20 8699 7527
www.wood4floors.co.uk

The Natural Wood Floors Co
+44 (0)20 8871 9771
www.naturalwoodfloor.co.uk

Raleo Surfaces
+1 212 206 1730
+1 800 697 1880
www.raleo.com

Walking on Wood
+44 (0)20 7352 7311
www.hardwoodfloors.co.uk

**The Wooden Floors Specialists
Ltd**
+44 (0)20 8675 2431
www.woodenfloors.co.uk

FABRIC

Abbott & Boyd Ltd
+44 (0)20 7351 9985
www.abbottandboyd.co.uk

Ainsworth-Noah
+1 404 231 8787
+ 1 800 669 3512
www.ainsworth-noah.com

Andrew Martin
+44 (0)20 7225 5100
+1 212 688 4498
www.andrewmartin.co.uk

Beacon Hill
+44 (0)1494 603 444
+1 800 343 1470
www.beaconhilldesign.com

Bergamo Fabrics
+1 914 665 0800
www.bergamofabrics.com

Boussac
+33 (0)1 44 77 36 00
www.boussacfadini.com

Brentano Inc
+1 847 657 8481
www.brentanofabrics.com

Brimar
+1 800 274 1205
www.brimarinc.com

Brunschwig & Fils, Inc.
www.brunschwig.com
+1 914 872 1100
+1 800 538 1880

Cabbages and Roses
+44 (0)20 7352 7333
www.cabbagesandroses.com

Carleton V
+1 212 355 4525

Chase Erwin silks
+44 (0)20 8875 1222
www.chase-erwin.com

Chelsea Textiles
+44 (0)20 7584 5544
www.chelseatextiles.com

Clarence House
+1 800 221 4704
+1 212 752 2890
www.clarencehouse.com

Cowtan & Tout
+1 310 659 1423

Création Baumann
+1 516 764 7431
+44 (0)20 7349 7022
www.creationbaumann.com

Dedar
+39 02 968 1381
+1 800 493 2209
www.dedar.com

De le Cuona
+44 (0)1753 830 301
www.delecuona.co.uk

Designers Guild
+44 (0)20 7893 7700
www.designersguild.com

Dominique Kieffer
+33 (0)1 42 21 32 44
www.dkieffer.com

Donghia
+1 212 925 2777
www.donghia.com

Eastern Accents
+1 800 397 4556
www.easternaccents.com

G P & J Baker
+44 (0)20 7351 7760
www.gpjbaker.com

Harlequin
+44 (0)8708 300 032
www.harlequin.uk.com

Jane Piper Reid & Company
+1 206 621 9290
www.jprco.com

Kelly Hoppen
+44 (0)20 7471 3350
www.kellyhoppen.com

Kravet, Inc.
+44 (0)20 7795 0110
www.kravet.com

Lee Jofa
+1 800 453 3563
www.leejofa.com

Lena Proudlock
+44 (0)1666 500 051
www.lenaproudlock.co.uk

Madura
+1 212 327 2681
+1 617 267 0222
www.madura.co.uk

Manuel Canovas
+33 (0)1 58 62 33 50
+44 (0)20 7351 0666
+1 212 647 6900
www.manuelcanovas.com

Nina Campbell
+44 (0)20 7225 1011
www.ninacampbell.com

Olivier Desforges
+1 800 322 3911
www.olivierdesforges.com

Osbourne & Little
+44 (0)20 7352 1456
+1 212 751 3333
www.osborneandlittle.com

Pindler & Pindler Inc
www.pindler.com
+1 805 531 9090
+1 800 669 6002

Pollack
+1 212 627 7766
www.pollackassociates.com

Rogers & Goffigon
+1 212 888 3242

Romo
+44 (0)1623 756 699
www.romofabrics.com

Rubelli
+39 041 2584 411
www.rubelli.com

Sahco Hesslein
+49 (0)911 99870
www.sahcohesslein.com

Sanderson
+44 (0)1895 830 044
+1 800 894 6185
www.sanderson-uk.com

Stark & Texture/Stark Carpet
+1 212 752 9000
+44 (0)20 7352 6001
www.starkcarpet.com

Storehouse
+1 888 786 7346
www.storehouse.com

Sun Atelier
+44 (0)20 890 3553
www.sunfabrics.com

Trade Routes
+44 (0)20 7622 6276

Travers & Company
+1 212 888 7900
www.traversinc.com

Turnell & Gigon
+44 (0)20 8971 1711
www.tandggroup.com

Zimmer + Rohde
+49 (0)617 163 202
+44 (0)20 7351 7115
+1 203 327 1400
www.zimmer-rohde.com

Zoffany
+44 (0)8708 300 060
+1 212 593 9787
+1 800 894 6185
www.zoffany.com

FAUX FUR

Andrew Martin
+44 (0)20 7225 5100
+1 212 688 4498
www.andrewmartin.co.uk

Brunschwig & Fils, Inc.
+1 914 872 1100
+1 800 538 1880
www.brunschwig.com

Christopher Hyland
+1 212 688 6121
www.christopherhyland.com

Clarence House
+1 800 221 4704
+1 212 752 2890
www.clarencehouse.com

Decorators Walk
+1 212 415 3955

Le Décor Français
+1 212 734 0032
www.ledecorfrancais.com

Duralee
+1 800 275 3872
www.duralee.com

Fonthill, Ltd
+1 212 755 6700
www.fonthill-ltd.com

F Schumacher & Co
+1 212 213 7717
+1 800 988 7775
www.fschumacher.com

J Robert Scott
+1 212 755 4910
+1 800 322 4910
www.jrobertscott.com

Nancy Corzine
+1 212 223 8340
www.nancycorzine.com

Osborne & Little
+44 (0)20 7352 1456
+1 212 751 3333
www.osborneandlittle.com

Scalamandré
+1 631 467 8800
+1 800 932 4361
www.scalamandre.com

Travers & Company
+1 212 888 7900
www.traversinc.com

LEATHER

African Light & Trading
+27 (21) 462 1490
www.altrad.co.za

Altiplano
+44 (0)20 7384 9371
www.altiplano.co.uk

Bauer International Inc
+1 800 582 7690
www.bauerinternational.com

Bernhardt
+44 (0)20 8882 7772
+1 (877) 205 5793
www.bernhardt.com

Elite Leather
www.eliteleather.com

Swaim
+1 336 885 6131
www.swaim-inc.com

Teddy & Arthur Edelman, Ltd
+1 212 751 3339
+1 800 886 TEDY
www.edelmanleather.com

FURNITURE

Artefacto
www.artefacto.com

Baker
+1 800 59-BAKER
www.bakerfurniture.com

Blanc d'Ivoire
www.blancdivoire.com

Bretz
+49 67 27 89 50
www.mycultsofa.com

Calico Corners
+1 800 213 6366
www.calicocorners.com

Decorative Crafts
+1 203 531 1500 or
+1 800 431 4455
www.decorativecrafts.com

Dedon
+49 (0) 41 31/22 44 7-0
www.dedon.de

Galerie Frédéric Méchiche
+33 (1) 42 78 78 28

Ixcasala
+33 (0)6 19 33 83 93
www.ixcasala.com

Janus et Cie
www.janusetcie.com

Ligne Roset
+1 800 BY ROSET
www.ligne-roset-usa.com
www.ligne-roset.co.uk

Ma Maison
+44 (0)20 7352 1181
www.mamaison.uk.com

Marianne von Kantzow
+46 8 663 9360
www.solgarden.net

McGuire
+1 800 662 4847
www.mcguirefurniture.com

Mitchell Gold & Bob Williams
+1 800 789 5401
www.mgandbw.com

Monkwell
+44 (0)20 7823 3294
www.monkwell.com

Newel
+1 212 758 1970
www.newel.com

Pamela Kline Traditions
+1 518 851 3975
www.traditionspamelakline.com

Robert Allen
+44 (0)1494 603 444
+1 800 333 3777
www.robertallendesign.com

Roche Bobois
+44 (0)20 7431 1411
www.roche-bobois.com

Smallbone of Devizes
+44 (0)20 7589 5998
+1 800 763 0096
www.smallbone.co.uk

Yves Delorme
+44 (0)20 7730 3435
+1 800 322 3911
www.yvesdelorme.com

ACCESSORIES

Artemide Lighting
+44 (0)20 8888 0001
+1 212 925 1588
www.artemide.com

Baccarat
+33 (0)8 20 32 22 22
www.baccarat.fr

Ballard Designs
+1 800 536 7551
www.ballarddesigns.com

Bellacor
+1 651 294 2500
+1 877 723 5522
www.shop.bellacor.com

Bill Amberg
+44 (0)20 7727 3560
www.billamberg.com

The Conran Shop
+44 (0)20 7589 7401
+1 212 755 9079
www.conranshop.co.uk

Contemporary Applied Arts
+44 (0)20 7436 2344
www.caa.org.uk

Crate & Barrel
+1 800 967 6696
www.crateandbarrel.com

The Dining Room Shop
+44 (0)20 8878 1020
www.thediningroomshop.co.uk

Fishs Eddy
www.fishseddy.com

Flos
+44 (0)20 7258 0600
+1 (0)516 549 2745
www.flos.com

Graham & Green
+44 (0)20 7727 4594
+44 (0)845 130 6622
www.grahamandgreen.co.uk

Guinevere Antiques
+44 (0)20 7736 2917
www.guinevere.co.uk

Habitat
+44 (0)20 7631 3880
+44 (0)845 601 0740
www.habitat.net

Harrison & Gil
+44 (0)1202 717 017
+44 (0)20 7348 7366
+1 239 939 9838
www.harrison-gil.com

Ikea
+44 (0)845 355 1141
+1 800 434 4532
www.ikea.com

Jane Sacchi Linens
+44 (0)20 7349 7020
www.janesacchi.com

Mathieu Lustrerie
+33 (0)4 90 74 92 40
www.mathieulustrerie.com

Piet Bone Zone at Mint
+44 (0)20 7224 4406

Pottery Barn
+1 888 779 5176
www.potterybarn.com

Restoration Hardware
1-800-910-9836
www.restorationhardware.com

Selfridges
+44 (0)8708 377 377
www.selfridges.com

Tade
+33 (0)4 94 62 19 41
www.tade.fr

Thomas Goode
+44 (0)20 7499 2823
www.thomasgoode.com

V V Rouleaux
+44 (0)20 7730 3125
www.vvrouleaux.com

West Elm
+1 888 922 4119
www.westelm.com

Zara Home
+44 (0)20 7590 6990
www.zarahome.com

FRAME

Aaron Brothers
+1 972 409 1300
+1 888 372 6464
www.aaronbrothers.com

Exposures
+1 800 222 4947
www.exposuresonline.com

Larson Juhl
+1 800 886 6126
www.larsonjuhl.com

DESIGNERS

Rachel Ashwell Design
+1 310 258 0660
www.shabbychic.com

Jason D Bell
+1 212 339 0006
www.jdbellinc.com

Louise Bradley
+44 (0)20 7589 1442
www.louisebradley.co.uk

Nancy Braithwaite Interiors Inc.
+1 404 355 1740

Alessandra Branca
+1 312 787 6123
www.branca.com

Sumien Brink
+27 (0)21 417 1168
Email: sbrinck@visi.co.za

Caproni Associates Inc.
+1 212 977 4010
caproni200@aol.com

David Carter
+44 (0)20 7790 0259
www.alacarter.com

Clodagh Design
+1 212 780 5755
www.clodagh.com

David Collins
+44 (0)20 7349 5900

Michael Coorengel &
Jean-Pierre Calvagrac
+33 (0)1 40 27 14 65
www.designdecoration.com

Bernie de le Cuona
+44 (0)1753 830 301
+44 (0)207 584 7677
www.delecuona.co.uk

Drake Design Associates
+1 212 754 3099
www.drakedesignassociates.com

Agnès Emery
+32 3 513 5892
www.emeryetcie.com

Luigi Esposito
+44 (0)20 7581 2500
www.formadesigns.co.uk

Gérard Faivre
+33 (0)4 90 95 98 50
www.gerardfaivre.com

Stephen Falcke
Fax: +27 (0)113 27 67 30

Frank Faulkner
+1 518 828 2295

Fox Linton Associates
+44 (0)20 7622 0920
www.foxlinton.co.uk

Terry Hunziker Inc.
+1 206 467 1144

Jacquelyne P Lanham
Designs
+1 404 364 0472

Jean Larette
www.larettedesign.com

Larry Laslo
+1 212 734 3824

Frédéric Méchiche
+33 (0)1 42 78 78 28

Catherine Memmi
+33 (0)1 44 07 22 28
+1 212 226 8200
www.catherinememmi.com

John Minshaw Designs
+44 (0)20 7486 5777

Eldo Netto
+1 212 888 7900

Alberto Pinto
+33 (0)1 40 13 75 80

Katharine Pooley
+44 (0)20 7584 3223
www.katharinepooley.com

Stephen Roberts
+1 212 966 6930
www.stephenroberts.com

Diana Sieff
+44 (0)20 7978 2422
www.sieff.co.uk

Vicente Wolf
+1 212 465 0590
www.vw-home.com

HOTELS

The G Hotel
+35 (0)3918 65200

The Grove Hotel
+44 (0)1923 807807
www.thegrove.co.uk

Home Hill Inn
+1 603 675 6165
www.homehillinn.com

Soho Hotel
www.sohohotel.com
+44 (0)20 7559 3000

Acknowledgements

THIS HAS BEEN A TRULY EXCITING BOOK TO WORK ON AND TO WRITE, as we have all felt we were breaking new ground rather than reinventing the wheel! As always, I have been given an enormous amount of assistance, encouragement and enthusiasm from so many people. I have my regular 'gang' in Walton Street without whose help I would not even contemplate a book – Bernie de le Cuona and her amazing team who closed the shop for a day in order that we could document her astonishing talent with texture and colour; Mona Perlhagen of Chelsea Textiles who has the perfect neutral sense of colour to a T; and everyone at Andrew Martin who found us wonderful fabric samples whenever we needed them and worked with us with enthusiasm and expertise; Katharine Pooley and Luigi Esposito, who were always willing to help in any way they could – but more about them later. What would I do without my Walton Street colleagues, not to mention Baker and Spice when we needed sustenance?

New and exciting ways of using colour in neutral palettes provided a challenge and we went to the innovative Kit Kemp at the Soho Hotel for inspiration and wonderful ideas. Luigi Esposito's design and Katharine Pooley's amazing accessorizing and the inspired concept of Waterside Penthouses gave us days of glorious photography. Francesca Wezel gave me endless information on how to succeed with the correct paint colours – such an important part of getting the look right. And Diana Sieff explained her winning ways with accenting neutrals for fabulous impact.

In New York Vicente Wolf and David Rogal were inspiring; Jamie Drake and Jason Witcher showed us how colour can be used in fascinating ways; Larry Laslo was his wonderful eclectic, eccentric, amazing self and gave me endless ideas, and Jason Bell was charming and as approachable as ever. Eldo Netto was as he always is – knowledgeable and full of enchanting ideas.

In Paris we had the joy of working with the talented and charismatic Michael Coorengel and Jean-Pierre Calvagrac in their stunning new apartment, and Gérard Faivre in his extraordinary tiny rue Bonaparte apartment, who showed us how you can create space with the right colours.

In South Africa Stephen Falcke allowed us to photograph three wonderful new homes he had designed, including the miraculous red house belonging to Adrian Brink. Sumien Brink of Cape Town, editor of the marvellous *Visi* magazine, gave us the benefit of her colour wisdom.

I would also like to thank Gerald Barrett and Caroline Kennedy of the G Hotel, who were amazingly helpful at all times.

We have had a great team working on this book and I want to thank them all for going the extra mile for me – I know I always ask just that little bit more! Luke White with whom I had not worked before but who very soon learnt to cope with my demanding ways! Chalkey Calderwood Pratt who managed to design the book from a great distance with energy, persistence and great talent. My very special editor Zia Mattocks – without her humour, persistence and enormous flair we would never have got this epic to bed. Of course, as always, it has been an enormous treat to work with Jacqui Small, who is the only person who can bully me into doing things I can't do!

Picture Credits

All photographs are by Luke White unless otherwise indicated.

Front endpaper: James Gager and Richard Ferretti's New York apartment designed in conjunction with Stephen Roberts;

Back endpaper: Colette's restaurant at The Grove, Hertfordshire, designed by Fox Linton Associates

1 Jamie Drake's East Hampton Home; 2–3 Catherine Memmi's house in Normandy; 4 a New York townhouse designed by Larry Laslo for LL Designs; 5 above Bernie de le Cuona's London showroom; 5 centre Gérard Faivre's apartment in Paris; 5 below a house in Bridgehampton designed by Vicente Wolf; 6 Bernie de le Cuona's Windsor house; 7 Catherine Memmi's house in Normandy; 8 a riverside apartment in London, designed by Luigi Esposito; 9 above the Soho Hotel, London designed by Kit Kemp; 9 below Bernie de le Cuona's Windsor house; 10 Michael Coorengel & Jean-Pierre Calvagrac's apartment in Paris; 11 a house in South Africa, designed by Stephen Falcke/photographer David Ross; 12 a New York penthouse loft designed by Clodagh Design; 13 Eldo Netto's apartment in New York; 14 a house in Bridgehampton designed by Vicente Wolf; 17 Kenneth Wyse's house in East Hampton designed by Larry Laslo for LL Designs; 18 James Gager and Richard Ferretti's New York apartment designed in conjunction with Stephen Roberts; 19 above Kenneth Wyse's house in East Hampton designed by Larry Laslo for LL Designs; 19 below a riverside apartment in London, designed by Luigi Esposito; 20 Bernie de le Cuona's Windsor house; 21 a house in Bridgehampton designed by Vicente Wolf; 22 Kenneth Wyse's house in East Hampton designed by Larry Laslo for LL Designs; 25 a riverside apartment in London, designed by Luigi Esposito; 26 a riverside apartment in London, designed by Luigi Esposito; 27 above Denise Seegal's apartment in New York, designed by Sonja & John Caproni/photographer Simon Upton; 27 below designer Alberto Pinto/photographer Giogio Baroni; 29 above a riverside apartment in London, designed by Luigi Esposito; 30 Mr & Mrs Robert Meyrowitz's Old Westbury house, designed by Vicente Wolf'; 32 above a New York townhouse designed by Larry Laslo of LL Designs; 32 below an apartment in New York, designed by Frédéric Méchiche/photographer Simon Upton; 33 Bernie de le Cuona's Windsor house; 34–35 a house in South Africa, designed by Stephen Falcke/photographer David Ross; 35 a house in South Africa, designed by Stephen Falcke/photographer David Ross; 36 above Frank Faulkner's house in Catskill, New York/photographer Simon Upton; 36 below a house in South Africa, designed by Stephen Falcke/photographer David Ross; 37 Bernie de le Cuona's Windsor house; 38 Bernie de le Cuona's Windsor house; 39 above a riverside apartment in London, designed by Luigi Esposito; 39 below a house in Watermill, designed by Vicente Wolf and his associate, David Rogal; 40 above Catherine Memmi's house in Normandy; 40 below left Bernie de le Cuona's Windsor house; 40 below right a riverside apartment in London, designed by Luigi Esposito; 41 above left Gérard Faivre's apartment in Paris; 41 above right a riverside apartment in London, designed by Luigi Esposito; 41 below Kenneth Wyse's house in East Hampton, designed by Larry Laslo for LL Designs; 42 Mr & Mrs Robert Meyrowitz's Old Westbury house, designed by Vicente Wolf; 45 designer Nancy Braithwaite/photographer Fritz von der Schulenburg; 46 Michael Coorengel & Jean-Pierre Calvagrac's apartment in Paris; 47 above Marianne von Kantzow's shop Solgården in Stockholm/photographer Simon Upton; 47 below a riverside apartment in London, designed by Luigi Esposito; 48 above Gérard Faivre's apartment in Paris; 48 below Frank Faulkner's house in Catskill, New York/photographer Simon Upton; 49 Denise Seegal's apartment in New York, designed by Sonja & John Caproni/photographer Simon Upton; 50–51 Mr & Mrs Robert Meyrowitz's Old Westbury house, designed by Vicente Wolf; 51 Michael Coorengael & Jean-Pierre Calvagrac's apartment in Paris/photographer Simon Upton; 52 The G Hotel, Galway, interior design by Philip Treacy; 55 a riverside apartment in London, designed by Luigi Esposito; 56 above Gérard Faivre's apartment in Paris; 56 below a riverside apartment in London, designed by Luigi Esposito; 57 a riverside apartment in London, designed by Luigi Esposito; 58 above The G Hotel, Galway, interior design by Philip Treacy; 58 below Michael Coorengel & Jean-Pierre Calvagrac's apartment in Paris; 59 Gérard Faivre's apartment in Paris; 60–64 a riverside apartment in London, designed by Luigi Esposito; 64–65 the Soho Hotel, London designed by Kit Kemp; 65 Michael Coorengael & Jean-Pierre Calvagrac's apartment in Paris/photographer Simon Upton; 66–67 James Gager and Richard Ferretti's New York apartment designed in conjunction with Stephen Roberts; 68 a New York townhouse, designed by Larry Laslo for LL Designs; 68 below Bernie de le Cuona's Windsor house; 69 above designer Stephanie Hoppen/photographer Fritz von der Schulenburg; 70 a riverside apartment in London, designed by Luigi Esposito; 70–71 Gérard Faivre's apartment in Paris; 71 James Gager and Richard Ferretti's New York apartment designed in conjunction with Stephen Roberts; 72 Jamie Drake's East Hampton home; 74 a house in Bridgehampton, designed by Vicente Wolf; 76 Mona Perlhagen of Chelsea Textiles' London showroom; 77 Agnès Emery's house in Brussels/photographer Simon Upton; 78 Marian Williams' New York apartment, designed by Jason D Bell; 81 interior by Jacquelynne P Lanham/photographer Simon Upton; 82 Mona Perlhagen of Chelsea Textiles' London showroom; 82–83 Denise Seegal's apartment in New York, designed by Sonja & John Caproni/photographer Simon Upton; 83 Marian Williams' New York apartment, designed by Jason D Bell; 84 above left & right interior by Jacquelynne P Lanham/photographer Simon Upton; 84 below Michael Coorengel & Jean-Pierre Calvagrac's apartment in Paris; 87 Pamela Kline (of Traditions)'s home in Claverack, New York/photographer Simon Upton; 88 left David Carter's house in London/photographer Simon Upton; 88 right Kenneth Wyse's house in East Hampton designed by Larry Laslo for LL Designs; 89 designer David Collins/photographer Fritz von der Schulenburg; 90 above Kenneth Wyse's house in East Hampton designed by Larry Laslo for LL Designs; 90 below Interior designer Terry Hunziker's Seattle apartment/photographer Ken Hayden; 92 David Carter's house in London/photographer Simon Upton; 93 above designer David Collins/photographer Fritz von der Schulenburg; 93 below Mona Perlhagen of Chelsea Textiles' London showroom; 95 Jamie Drake's East Hampton home; 96 Michael Coorengel and Jean-Pierre Calvagrac's apartment in Paris/photographer Simon Upton; 98 left Eldo Netto's apartment in New York; 98 right Colette's Restaurant at The Grove, Hertfordshire, designed by Fox Linton Associates; 99 designer Alberto Pinto/photographer Giorgio Baroni; 100 above left Jamie Drake's East Hampton home; 100 above right Eldo Netto's apartment in New York; 100 below Michael Coorengel & Jean-Pierre Calvagrac's apartment in Paris; 102 Noel Berk and Omedes' New York apartment, designed by Drake Design Associates; 104 Bernie de le Cuona's Windsor house; 105 Noel Berk and Omedes' New York apartment, designed by Drake Design Associates; 106 Mona Perlhagen of Chelsea Textiles' London showroom; 107 above Deborah Brett's London home/photographer Bob Smith; 107 below an apartment in New York designed by Frédéric Méchiche/photographer Simon Upton; 108 Lena Proudlock of Denim In Style's house in Gloucestershire/photographer Simon Upton; 109 Bernie de le Cuona's London showroom; 111 Colette's restaurant at The Grove, Hertfordshire, designed by Fox Linton Associates; 112 Jamie Drake's East Hampton home; 112–113 a house in South Africa, designed by Stephen Falcke/photographer David Ross; 113 The G Hotel, Galway, interior design by Philip Treacy; 114 above Colette's restaurant at The Grove, Hertfordshire, designed by Fox Linton Associates; 114 below Elena & Stephen Georgiadis' London house, designed by John Minshaw Designs Limited/photographer Simon Upton; 115 a riverside apartment in London, designed by Luigi Esposito; 116 above Jamie Drake's East Hampton home; 116 below a house in South Africa, designed by Stephen Falcke/photographer David Ross; 117 Colette's restaurant at The Grove, Hertfordshire, designed by Fox Linton Associates; 118 the Soho Hotel, London designed by Kit Kemp; 121 Jamie Drake's East Hampton home; 122 Bernie de le Cuona's London showroom; 123 Jamie Drake's East Hampton home/photographer Fritz von der Schulenburg; 124 The G Hotel, Galway, interior design by Philip Treacy; 125 the Soho Hotel, London designed by Kit Kemp; 126–130 a house in South Africa, designed by Stephen Falcke/photographer David Ross; 133 the Soho Hotel, London designed by Kit Kemp; 134 designer Louise Bradley/photographer Ray Main; 135 Gérard Faivre's apartment in Paris; 136 the Soho Hotel, London designed by Kit Kemp; 138 Jamie Drake's East Hampton home; 139 above The G Hotel, Galway, interior design by Philip Treacy; 139 below the Soho Hotel, London designed by Kit Kemp; 140 Noel Berk and Omedes' New York apartment, designed by Drake Design Associates; 143 photographer Simon Upton; 144 Denise Seegal's apartment in New York, designed by Sonja & John Caproni/photographer Simon Upton; 144–145 Jerry & Maxine Swartz's house in Germantown, designed by Frank Faulkner/photographer Simon Upton; 145 photographer Simon Upton; 146 designer Nancy Braithwaite/photographer Fritz von der Schulenburg; 148 Jamie Drake's East Hampton home; 150 Bernie de le Cuona's Windsor house; 151 the Soho Hotel, London designed by Kit Kemp; 152 Jerry & Maxine Swartz's house in Germantown, designed by Frank Faulkner/photographer Simon Upton; 153 Michael Coorengel & Jean-Pierre Calvagrac's apartment in Paris; 154 Jeannette Chang's apartment in New York, designed by Sonja & John Caproni/photographer Simon Upton; 156 Stephane & Victoria du Roure's home in New Hampshire/photographer Simon Upton; 157 above Bernie de le Cuona's Windsor house; 157 below Jerry & Maxine Swartz's house in Germantown, designed by Frank Faulkner/photographer Simon Upton; 158–161 a New York penthouse loft designed by Clodagh Design; 162 Mr & Mrs Robert Meyrowitz's Old Westbury house, designed by Vicente Wolf; 163 a New York townhouse designed by Larry Laslo for LL Designs; 164–165 a New York penthouse loft designed by Clodagh Design; 166 Eldo Netto's apartment in New York; 168 designer Alberto Pinto/photographer Giorgio Baroni; 169 Mr & Mrs Robert Meyrowitz's Old Westbury house, designed by Vicente Wolf; 170 above a riverside apartment in London, designed by Luigi Esposito; 170 below a New York townhouse designed by Larry Laslo for LL Designs; 173 a house in Watermill, designed by Vicente Wolf and his associate, David Rogal; 174 a New York townhouse designed by Larry Laslo for LL Designs; 175 above the Soho Hotel, London designed by Kit Kemp; 175 below a house in South Africa, designed by Stephen Falcke/photographer David Ross; 176 Bernie de le Cuona's London showroom; 177 the Soho Hotel, London designed by Kit Kemp; 179 a riverside apartment in London, designed by Luigi Esposito; 180 a house in South Africa, designed by Stephen Falcke/photographer David Ross; 181 above a riverside apartment in London, designed by Luigi Esposito; 181 below left a riverside apartment in London, designed by Luigi Esposito; 181 below right designer Alberto Pinto/photographer Giorgio Baroni; 182 above a riverside apartment in London, designed by Luigi Esposito; 182 below Bernie de le Cuona's London showroom; 183 Noel Berk and Omedes' New York apartment, designed by Drake Design Associates.

Index